A Brief History of
Red Hook
CLARE O'NEILL CARR

August 20, 2002

To Greta,

Hope you enjoy this brief history of your grandfather's adopted small town.... we are very glad, by the way, to have adopted him. AND you too!

All the best

Clare O'Neill Carr

THE WISE FAMILY TRUST
in cooperation with
The Egbert Benson Historical Society of Red Hook

Acknowledgments

This short history was made possible through the work of a number of devoted recorders of history, living and dead, whom I am very glad to finally have the opportunity to acknowledge and thank: First, the late John and Clara Losee, who, for years, meticulously recorded, collected and catalogued deeds, diaries, photographs and family histories out of pure enjoyment and interest. Their life-time collections form a major part of the Egbert Benson Historical Society's archives at the Elmendorph Inn, which I used extensively; the late Red Hook Village Historian, Rosemary Coons, whose collections, as well as whose indefatigable spirit, are reflected in these pages; the late William Teator, local farmer, naturalist, artist and fervent recorder of day-to-day life in turn-of-the-century Red Hook, whose photographs, preserved in glass plate negatives, are a treasure; the late Harriet Martin Dey, a woman who grew up at the historic Martin house, and whose camera recorded scenes of life here in the late 1890s; and Fred Briggs, whose extensive postcard collection, carefully gathered over a lifetime, has caught and preserved so much of the history of the town. The Losee, Coon, Teator and Dey collections are in the EBHSRH archives.

The development of this book was especially inspired and sustained by the following people, to whom I am most grateful: J. Winthrop Aldrich, the Red Hook Town Historian, who generously loaned material and photographs from his Rokeby collection and read the manuscript several times, and without whose extensive knowledge and passion for this town's history, this book would not have been made possible; Barbara Bielenberg, the president of the Egbert Benson Historical Society, whose encouragement and advice often kept me going; Barbara Thompson, whose knowledge of the collections at the Red Hook historical society, and willingness to help me in hunting out the details and photographs, made my job so much easier; Richard Wiles, former editor of the Hudson Valley Regional Review and Charles Ranlett Flint Professor Emeritus of Economics at Bard College, who over the years has taught me how to seek out the true history of a community by looking at how ordinary people lived, worked and made their living; My husband, Geoffrey Carr, and our children, who always supported me; and, with special gratitude, *About Town* editor Paul DeAngelis of Tivoli, who agreed to edit my manuscript at several crucial junctures when cutting was essential and I was desperate for direction.

I also want to thank the following: To Maynard Ham, who lent his time, as well as his wonderful pictures and material; Cynthia Philip, who read over my manuscript and made some very important suggestions, as did Jane Gottlieb; Annys Wilson, the librarian in charge of historic archives at Bard College; Sidney Mead and Sid Delanoy, who shared many stories of Upper Red Hook; Upper Red Hook historian, the Reverend Roger Leonard; Karen and Dave Fraleigh, whose family albums span over 100 years; Alice Bulkeley, Ellen and James Hogan, Keith Denegar, Pat Asher, Arnold Colburn, Stanton Tremper Jr. and Don Triebel, and historical archeologist Christopher Lindner of Bard College; Rhinebeck Town Historian Nancy Kelly, who retrieved some very important documentation for me of the Beekman allotments from Princeton University Library; Emma Coon, who is a fountain of knowledge; Robert Ludwig, Richard King, photographer Tom Daley, Donna Matthews, Tivoli historians Bernie Tieger and Tom Cordier; the Montgomery Place staff, Lucy Kuriger and Geoffrey Carter; Bruce Naramore and staff of Clermont Historic Site; historian Bill McDermott of Clinton, who is ever generous with his time and knowledge of early Dutchess County; and for all those whom I may have omitted who dug into their records or their closets and tapped their memories for photographs and stories of this town and its institutions, my great thanks.

My special appreciation goes to Len Vogler, my book designer, who has endless patience and great skill; Herman Gorgens, man at the front, for all the hours spent coordinating meetings, dates and deadlines, and for listening to my tales of woe. A special thanks goes to Duke Vicks of Vicks Lithograph and Printing Corporation. Last, but not least, my sincere gratitude, and that of the Egbert Benson Historical Society of Red Hook, goes to the publisher, Robert Wise, who, fortunately for us, creates beautiful books for a living, whose interest in the town was the initiating and driving force behind this project and whose generous support made the book possible.

All proceeds from the sale of this book will go to the Egbert Benson Historical Society of Red Hook

Project manager and interior design: Len Vogler

Cover design by Chloe Alexander

The cover illustration is a detail from the mural in the Rhinebeck Post Office painted by: Olin Dows

US International Standard Book Number: 0-8256-9422-1

Reorder from:
THE WISE FAMILY TRUST
257 Park Avenue South
New York, NY 10010

printed in the United States of America by
Vicks Lithograph and Printing Corporation

Chapter 1
Beneath the Blue Mountains

*t*he Heermance homestead, an early Dutch house, stands today behind a row of century-old locust trees along West Kerley's Corners Road in the Town of Red Hook. It is built of stone, with a wide double Dutch door facing south. Its small-paned windows sparkle in the sun. Beyond the meadows and hay fields to the west, the Catskill Mountains rise up dramatically, extending their sweep north and south above the Hudson Valley. In all seasons, and at almost all points, these mountains dominate the landscape of the town. Referring to the strikingly deep hue of the peaks in winter, early settler David Van Ness described his Red Hook home as "beneath the blue mountains." [1]

The Heermance/Bulkeley House: One of the earliest houses in town, it was built on West Kerleys Corners Road in Upper Red Hook in the early 18th century by the Heermances. They were listed in 1750 as pathmasters for their road, which led from the inland farms to the river at upper Red Hook landing. The Locust trees, planted over 100 years ago to shade horses and wagons, once lined the road to Tivoli. Trees and farmhouse are on the National Registor of Historic Places. Photo by Douglas Baz.

Andries Heermance was among the first to settle in this part of the valley, in what is now Red Hook. His family emigrated from Holland in the late 17th century. In 1724, Heermance partnered with Barent Van Benthuysen, another Dutchman from Kingston, to buy 1000 acres of what was to become Upper Red Hook. His son built the stone house sometime before 1755, placing it along a path leading from the Hudson River landing (later called Tivoli). The path led eastward to the nearby Post Road and beyond to Connecticut and the New England colonies. The Van Benthuysens lived near the river at Annandale, on the road leading to Cruger's Island, giving rise to the pattern of settlement along both river and highway that has continued to this day.

The Gotlieb Martin/Cookingham House: Built in the summer of 1776 by Gotlieb (sometimes spelled Gottlop) Martin for his newly married son, the stuccoed stone house remained in the Martin family until Oakleigh Cookingham bought the farm in 1933. The cornerstone was laid July 4, 1776. It is said that a small contingent of Continental soldiers passed by the old Post Road as the frame was being raised that summer, dropped their gear and lent a hand. Harriet Martin Dey Collection.

Quite a number of early American houses remain in Red Hook. The Catskills form the backdrop to the Mohr farmhouse, a neat clapboard cottage with fieldstone and brick additions surrounded by a meadow along River Road. German immigrant Phillip Heinrich Mohr built it just one mile from the river landing that would later be called Barrytown.

3

In the Village of Red Hook, the Gottlieb and Heinrich Martin stone houses stand near the town's first millstream, the Saw Kill. The oldest was constructed 25 years before the Revolutionary War; the latest was said to have gone up on Independence Day, July 4, 1776. The *c.*1750 Elmendorph Inn, an old stagecoach stop rescued from destruction in the 1970s, still sits close to the Old Post Road (State Route 9) in Red Hook Village; and Montgomery Place, a grand house and built landscape that overlook the Hudson at Annandale, remains as one example of the dozen "Great Estates" that rose along Red Hook's waterfront between 1794 and 1915.

These structures remain as evidence of the unusual mix of Europeans—Dutch, English, French Huguenots, Irish and Germans—who settled almost 300 years ago in the five hamlets of Red Hook, in what was then called the north ward of the Dutchess Precinct of Rhinebeck.

The Place

View from Montgomery Place: *This small oil painting, artist unknown, portrays the striking view from* Mongtgomery Place *in Annandale, looking northwest to the Hudson and Catskills beyond. Painted in 1854, the recently arrived Hudson River Railroad, so obtrusive to some at the time, is tactfully hidden.* Rokeby Collection.

Dominated by striking blue mountains, run through with two generous streams, the town is a series of high ridges and plains that eventually fall to the Hudson River on the west. On one of the plains is the primary Village of Red Hook. Another plain, to the northeast, near the hamlet of Upper Red Hook, contains some of the best farmland in New York State, on which are set out large fruit and vegetable farms with a scattering of sheep and beef cattle. Red Hook is bounded by the high hills of the Town of Milan, its neighbor to the east; and by the stream, Steen Valetje, a Dutch name meaning "little stony falls," on the border of the Town of Rhinebeck, its neighbor to the south. Route 9, a major road once called the King's Highway, cuts through the town, north and south. Near its northern boundary, at the Columbia County line, runs the White Clay Kill, an old millstream that passes through the incorporated Village of Tivoli. Tivoli, overlooking the Hudson River at North Bay, is one of two riverside hamlets in the town, the other being Barrytown four miles to the south.

The larger of the two millstreams, both of which served the town for 200 years, is the Saw Kill, which the Native American Indians called Metambesem. It flows through the central part of town on its way to the Hudson, at the hamlet of Annandale. Two lakes on the eastern border first appeared on original 17th century patent deeds: the larger, Long Lake (now called Spring Lake), and the smaller, a deep glacial pond, which the Indians called Wanaughkameek. From almost every settlement and well-traveled road in this town of more than 10,000, you can see the Catskill Mountains rising up to the west. The effect can be striking. In picture postcards of the 1920s and 1930s, Red Hook was celebrated for its beautiful sunsets, which dip below the "deep blue mountains" in the distance.

The population is dispersed among two incorporated villages and three hamlets, all of which have their origins in the 18th century, and in a half dozen housing developments, built in the 20th century. Red Hook is home to Bard College, a well-respected, private liberal arts college that grew up with the town. Large tracts of land along the Hudson protect Red Hook's shoreline from commercial development, a reminder of a land-grant system put in place three centuries ago. In the countryside, working fruit and vegetable farms still exist in this once primarily agricultural community and are a main contributor to the economy. They can be found now, side by side with new houses built on former pastureland, inhabited by citizens who mainly commute to jobs outside town.

The Beginnings

By the time the Heermances made their mark on history at West Kerley's Corners in the first quarter of the 18th century, more than one hundred years had passed since Henry Hudson had arrived in the Town of Red Hook. The legendary English explorer was the first European to claim the land and to name it.

In the fall of 1609, under contract to the Dutch West India Company, he sailed his ship the *Half Moon* (*Halve Moen*) up the broad river that would later carry his name, in his quest to find a western passage to the East Indies. Hudson anchored near Cruger's Island on the evening of September 15, 1609.

There he drew in fresh water for his hopeful voyage, "caught a great store of very good fish," and was met by Native American Indians riding out in their canoes to greet his crew. He later described the natives in his ships log as: "very loving people, and very old men," by whom he was "very well used." The natives brought Indian corn, pumpkins and tobacco, which they exchanged for "trifles."[2] The *Half Moon* lingered for a day and two nights. The island, really a peninsula at low tide, was turning autumn red

Henry Hudson's Haelve Moen: A Watercolor rendering of the Half Moon by H.J. Kohler presented to the 1909 New York State Hudson-Fulton Celebration Commission. A replica of the Dutch ship sailed up the Hudson that year to commemorate the 300th anniversary of Hendrick Hudson's discovery of the river. The dual celebration also honored the 100th anniversary of Robert Fulton's steamboat invention by sailing a replica of the Clermont. *The Hudson-Fulton Celebration, 1909, Vol. I, Albany, J.B. Lyon Co., 1910.*

from its dense growth of sumac and Virginia creeper. Noting the shade and shape of the headland, the sailors called it "Roed Hoeck," the Dutch name for Red Hook. The *Half Moon* never found the western passage, but Hudson claimed the new colony for the company under the flag of Holland. The Dutch West India company erected forts on the Hudson at New Amsterdam, Wiltwyck and Beverwyck, named by the British after 1664, New York, Kingston and Albany respectively. The Dutch were interested in protecting their commercial interests, mainly in the lucrative beaver pelt trade, against the French and Indians, and little settlement took place that century.

Shad Harvest: A pen and ink drawing of Delaware Indians fishing and preparing shad in early spring along the river. A fishweir consisting of wooden stakes arranged in a fence-like manner, and weighted fish net, are being used to gather the shad so that they may be easily speared or caught with bare hands. A previous catch of fish has already been gutted, split and placed near a fire-hearth and over racks to dry for storage. Shad ascended the Hudson by the millions in March and April to spawn and were a major source of food for the local Indians. In the 19th century the annual run of the delicious fish and its equally valuable roe, became a major source of business for fishermen in Red Hook. Drawing by John C. Kraft, from The Lenape, or Delaware Indians by Herbert C. Kraft, Seton Hall University Museum, South Orange, N.J., 1987.

The presence of native peoples in the Hudson Valley has been traced back 11,000 years. In Red Hook there is evidence of seasonal camps dating back at least 4,000 years. At the time of Hudson's visit, the town was sparsely inhabited by Mahican Indians, Algonquian-speaking people and part of the far-branching Delaware tribe, who lived along the coast and inland from Chesapeake Bay to the Roeliff Jansen Kill. In this part of the Hudson Valley, local groups were called the Wappingers, the Sepascots and, across the river, the Esopus. The Wappingers ranged from Putnam County to Columbia County. They hunted and fished in the Hudson Valley, and traded with the Iroquois Five Nations to the west. They lived in houses made of bark and trees, and they cultivated beans, squash, pumpkins and corn in small settlements. In spring they fished for shad in the Hudson, drying their catch on the shore to store for winter. Archaeologists have uncovered evidence of these early camps, as well as evidence of tools and weapons manufactured there for trade, at Bard College campus, near the same Cruger's Island where Hudson weighed anchor almost 400 years ago.

For almost 100 years, the tribes who first greeted Hudson on that autumn day in 1609 saw little of the Europeans on the eastern shore of the river. But it was not long after European settlement of Red Hook began in the first decades of the 1700s that the Native Americans' claims to their land would be entirely wiped out through the systematic "buying" of the land, by both Dutch and English landlords. In fact, the price they paid for vast tracts of this fertile and richly forested land often amounted to little more than muskets, whiskey, cloth and trinkets.

Beginning in the late 17th century, Europeans, mostly Dutch, purchased land from local tribes throughout the Hudson Valley, including Red Hook, then arranged for patents to be issued through the English colonial governors, thereby legalizing their title to the land. These were mostly absentee landlords, and actual settlement followed slowly. The vast land holdings, which were established along the Hudson from New York to Albany, would influence the development of communities like Red Hook for years to come.

In the meantime, as Europeans encroached upon their traditional hunting and fishing grounds, the native peoples moved out of the region, their numbers finally declining to the point of extinction by the end of the 18th century.

In 1895, local farmer John Lewis spoke to a group of students at St. Stephen's Theological Seminary in the Red Hook hamlet of Annandale, about the last Native American Indians in Red Hook. A small Native American Indian settlement overlooking North Bay on the Hudson, known as Red Man's Corner, had gradually died out, "until… they disappeared before the march of civilization," wrote Lewis. He added, "The last two of whom we have any account died on our farm (in Annandale) in my father's lifetime."[3]

The Dutch and English periods were a time of trade and settlement. Settlers like the Mohrs and Heermances took advantage of the opportunities offered from the vast amount of unsettled land in the Hudson Valley. The occasional claims of the Native American Indians for the land's return, filed in federal and state courts quite early in the life of the new Republic, would not have impressed them. Like John Lewis, 150 years later, they felt that civilization, by definition, belonged only to them.

Chapter 2
The English Arrive

*U*nder Dutch rule, Red Hook remained completely unsettled by Europeans. Activity was centered at the trading posts of New Amsterdam (New York City), Esopus (Kingston) and Fort Orange (Albany), where the fur and beaver skin trade dominated. The land was thickly forested and difficult to clear for farming. Vast tracts of land to the north and south, called patroonships, were controlled by Dutch landowners who encouraged some clearing and settlement of the land through leasing, on strict, almost feudal, terms. However, little settlement occurred. That changed when the English took over the colony in 1664. In a bloodless coup, they sailed into New Amsterdam and forced a Dutch surrender. The English began to push for settlement of New York for both political and economic reasons. Vital, populated communities were important to the authorities in England, as well as to the governors in the colonies, in order to resist French encroachment in America. It was also important to establish a strong farming economy to replace the disappearing beaver trade, as the small animals with their fine, silky pelts had been hunted and trapped almost to extinction by the 1700s.

While Dutch patroons, like Killiaen Van Rensselaer near Albany, hastened to secure their vast holdings under English rule, the British Crown extended the land grant system. James II of England granted ownership of large tracts of land along the Hudson to those individuals, or groups of individuals, either influential or clever enough to claim them. For this favor, the colonial government received a yearly, modest quitrent from the landlords, and, most importantly, their political loyalty. In the Hudson Valley, men like Judge Henry Beekman Sr., a Dutchman from Kingston, were issued patents that granted ownership and control over all land, water and mineral rights. Beekman was granted a patent for much of the land around Rhinebeck, to the south of Red Hook, on April 22, 1697.

The English granted manors (similar to the Dutch patroonships), which awarded feudal entitlements like the kind found in 17th-century Europe. In 1686, Scotsman Robert Livingston, whose family would later play a significant role in the development of the town, was granted a 160,000-acre manor adjacent to Red Hook in the north. Indeed, until 1799, Red Hook's borders encompassed the small portion of the Clermont part of that manor. Clermont was the home of Chancellor Robert Livingston, an important American statesman in the Colonial and Federal periods, a drafter of the Declaration of Independence and the first Chancellor of New York State.

Red Hook's First Landowners

The first European to own land in Red Hook was Colonel Pieter Schuyler. Schuyler was a Dutchman, and the first mayor of the City of Albany. On June 2, 1688, he was granted from King James II a patent south of Livingston's manor that included what was to become 125 years later, the entire town of Red Hook. The land was bounded in the north by the manor line near Tivoli; in the south, by the stream, Steen Valetje; to the west, by the Hudson River; and to the east, by Spring Lake and by Wanaughkameek (near the hamlet of Rock City, on the border of Milan.) Schuyler never lived there, and the land was not settled until a quarter of a century later.

Soon after he secured his patent, Schuyler sold off all his Red Hook lands, dividing them into "Great Lots." The fellow Dutchmen to whom he sold them became, in turn, the patentees. Colonel Henry Beekman Jr., the son of the founder of Rhinebeck, bought 5500 acres of the southern portion of Schuyler's Red Hook lands in 1715 from one of the Dutchman, Peek DeWitt. These he added to his extensive holdings inherited from his father in the present day Town of Rhinebeck.

Colonel Pieter Schuyler: This prominent Dutchman, and first mayor of Albany, was granted a patent on June 2, 1688 from King James II for land that covered what would later become the entire town of Red Hook. He never lived here. Collection of the City of Albany, Office of the Major.

His patent line was extended north to the Saw Kill and included what is now the Village of Red Hook. Beekman became the largest single landowner in Red Hook. By 1725, the balance of Schuyler's patent was divided among five Dutch men: Barent Van Benthuysen (his line ran from the Saw Kill to the north of Cruger's Island, and included large holdings eastward to Spring Lake), Barent Staats, Lowrance Knickerbacker and his brothers, H. Gansevoort and Nicholas Hoffman (his purchase encompassed the area of the Village of Tivoli). [4]

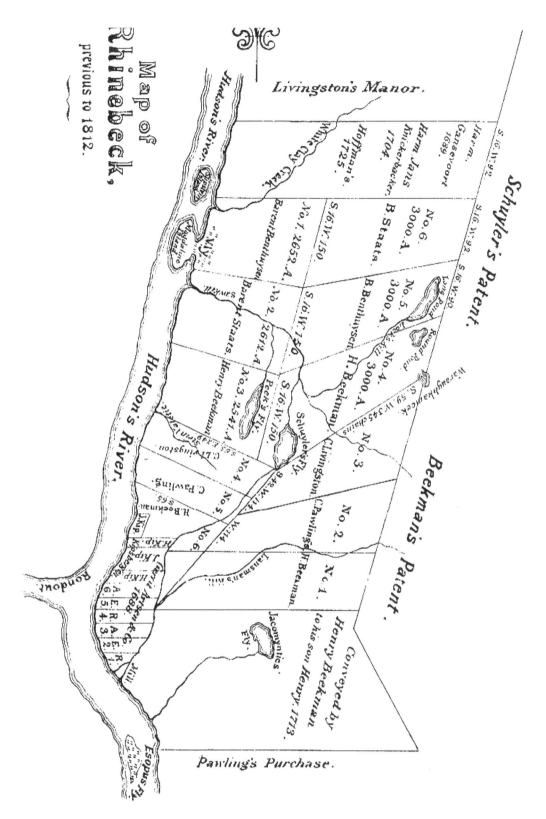

Great Lots: By 1721, Schuyler's patent had been divided into seven "Great Lots" and resold. This early drawing of Rhinebeck, which included Red Hook and parts of Staatsburg until 1812, shows the disposition of Schuyler's lands and the major landowners in Red Hook after 1721: Beekman, Van Benthuysen, Staats, Knickerbacker, and Hoffman. EBHSRH Achrives.

Chapter 3
Red Hook Develops Its First Communities

In order to settle these large tracts of uncleared land and make them productive, the landowners leased their land to tenant farmers in lots of between 25 and 200 acres. The terms of the leases sometimes were secured "forever," or for at least two and three generations, while the landlords retained title to the land and mineral and mill rights to the streams. The patentees exacted rents in the form of scheppels and bushels of wheat and "fat hens to be delivered each year on May 1st, the feast of the Annunciation of the Blessed Virgin Mary, commonly called Lady Day." They also paid with "days riding," a system that required the tenant to provide his horse and several days free labor at the landlord's bidding—often to improve or maintain roads, bridges and other community amenities.[5] Tenants were responsible for clearing the land of trees and stumps, planting and harvesting crops and building their barns (which usually went up first) and their houses, as well as their own roads and bridges. They paid local property taxes and were responsible for managing, maintaining and improving their farms. The wheat they grew had to be ground at their landlord's mill and shipped on his sloops.

"The Scheme of Division of Part of the Estate of Mrs. Margaret Livingston of Claremont at New York, and in the Counties of Dutchess and Ulster:" The seventh lot, Red Hook, was drawn by Alida Livingston and contains a list of original tenants, their acreage, dates and terms of their leases, and their annual rents in scheppels of wheat, "fat hens" and "days riding." Some of the earliest lessee names, such as Lown, Feller, Mowl and Klum, can still be found in Red Hook. Edward Livingston Papers, Firestone Library, Princeton University, Princeton, N.J.

In return, the landlord would often finance the early years of establishing the farm, usually seven years, or see the tenants through years of bad weather or natural disaster when few crops were harvested. This unfortunately often kept tenants in arrears for years. Leases were passed down within the family, or sold, with the landlord's permission. He would have first refusal to buy the lease, and would pay the farmer for any improvements to the property, that is, buildings, bridges, barns, etc. He would also set the price.

In the Hudson Valley, this system attracted adventurous men and women who were prompted to emigrate from the increasingly crowded countries of Western Europe. They put their hands to work clearing and cultivating what was then virgin forest. They secured the rights to the land and to the living it yielded for generations. Plus they created communities and a strong citizenry.

However, there was little opportunity to buy land and expand their farms. Men, who in 1776 had left their farms to fight for independence for their fledgling country, returned to their Hudson Valley farms to realize that there was no hope of financial independence for themselves in their own community. In the 18th century, rent wars plagued the land grants adjacent to Red Hook in Columbia County and to the south in Westchester, where patroons and manor lords exercised even stricter control over the lives of their tenants than did the local patentees. It was not until 1842, following the bloodiest rent wars in the 1820s, that the perpetual lease was finally outlawed by the New York State Legislature.

Henry Beekman, "Farmer"

Henry Beekman. Historic Old Rhinebeck, Howard H. Morse, 1908.

Conditions for the tenant farmer were better in 18th century Red Hook/Rhinebeck, and most of the patentees were traditionally lenient in the terms of their leases. Farms were a little larger, which meant more wheat production (wheat was the primary crop since it was demanded as rent, in bushels or, sometimes, in the equivalent in shillings and pounds). Also, rents were easier. For example rent was 14 bushels of wheat per year on an average 153-acre farm in Beekman's patent, compared to 19 bushels from an average 84-acre farm in Livingston's Manor.[6] An English visitor to Clermont in 1794 found with some surprise "more of the spirit of feudal aristocracy," than he had expected to find in the land of leaders of a Republic.[7]

In contrast, Henry Beekman Jr., Red Hook's largest landowner, and one of the richest men in the area, identified himself as "farmer" on the early censuses, not "gentleman" as the Livingstons did. He had a reputation for being evenhanded with his tenants, and could at times be lenient, even forgiving their debt.

Although, under the terms of the land grant, the Red Hook patentees were not required to sell their land, they sometimes did so. This created small freeholds among the primarily leased farms that prevailed in Red Hook/Rhinebeck.

The First Settlers

The first to actually settle the land in Red Hook were German farmers who came to the area in the first half of the 18th century. Tripling the meager population with their presence, they left perhaps the strongest imprint on the ethnic makeup of Red Hook and Rhinebeck people, an influence that is seen today in the names of its citizens. In 1710, the first wave of German Palatines arrived in Germantown under a scheme by the British Crown to produce pine pitch, spars and caulking for the Royal Navy. Striking a deal with Robert Livingston, the first lord of the Livingston Manor, the crown agreed to pay passage of several hundred families from the German Palatinate to the colonies, in exchange

Mohr House, *Barrytown: Philip Heinrich Mohr, a Palatine immigrant, built this stone and clapboard farmhouse on a freehold he bought from Barent Van Benthuysen in 1732.* Losee Collection.

for work in the colonies. The Germans had already been marooned in England as refugees, where they had fled to escape the warring and bad weather conditions at home, as well as religious persecution. They were to be settled in lands north of Red Hook, at East Camp, later named Germantown after their homeland. Another group settled across the river in West Camp. The pine pitch manufacture was a failure, however, partly because the area did not have the proper trees for the production. Unfortunately, the winters of 1710 and 1711 were terrible, and the English authorities did not make good on their promise to feed, shelter and clothe the refugees. However the experiment established the German presence in the region.

In 1714, at the invitation of patentee Henry Beekman, about 35 families moved south to Red Hook and Rhinebeck after spending several harsh and hungry winters at Germantown. Beekman provided them with land for a church and farms to lease on sometimes-generous terms. Records show that the Palatines signed leases to farm Beekman lands in Red Hook, beginning with Carol Neher in 1718 and continuing through to the Revolutionary War. A few Palatines, like Phillip Mohr in Barrytown, bought land outright. Most others, like Valentine Bender (Benner), Nicholas Bonesteel and Carol Neher, leased their farms. These were the families who, along with Dutch pioneers like Heermance, Vosburgh, Knickerbacker and Widbeck, first cleared the land, built the barns and stone walls and fenced the livestock.

The first pioneers settled around the river landings and the mills in Tivoli, Barrytown and Annandale. The landings and mill sites gave access to the water and the landlords became the town's first freighters, millers and ferrymen.

Life in the Rhinebeck/Red Hook area was pretty simple and attached to the seasonal rhythms of the farm and the crops—even in the wealthier households. Much of the correspondence between Margaret Beekman Livingston and her husband, Robert (The Judge) of Clermont, had to do with the farm, the slaves, the problems with the Palatines, crops and household details. Farm life for the poorer tenant farmers could be hard and dull.

The First Community: The Hoffmans and Tivoli Landing

Hoffman's "Castle:" This grand stone house was built by Martin Hoffman in about 1760 close to the family's enterprises at Hoffman's Mills. The Hoffmans helped develop Tivoli, the earliest community in town. The house no longer exists. Fred Briggs Collection.

Tenant farms were scattered around the Red Hook area from the early 1700s, but it appears that the Hoffmans were the first to develop a settled community in Red Hook. Nicholas Hoffman bought land near Tivoli from Pieter Schuyler in 172l. He built a landing and established the first ferry in Red Hook. Hoffman purchased from the original Schuyler patent most of what would become the Village of Tivoli—that portion that lay between the White Clay Kill and Livingston's manor. His sons, Martin, Anthony, Zacharias and Petrus, developed the early settlement, known as the upper Red Hook landing or Hoffman's Ferry. They built a river ferry and wharf at the foot of Sycamore Point, a high bluff overlooking the river at North Bay. By mid-century, they had established a mill at the mouth of the White Clay Kill. (Later, it was burned by the British but was not rebuilt.) Nearby, Martin built a substantial stone house above his dock overlooking the Hudson, that has since disappeared.

Martin and Nicholas were both listed as landowners in the census of Dutchess County in 1740. Although Nicholas was said not to have ever lived in Red Hook, there is evidence that by that year his sons had made Tivoli their home.

By the end of the century, the Hoffmans moved inland, establishing a complex of barns and houses, as well as a milling operation northeast of Tivoli village where Route 9G now crosses the stream. These buildings, all painted red, became a local landmark, and Tivoli was referred to as Hoffman's Mills. By the 19th century, the family had built a mill at the southwest corner of the Broadway Bridge and another further north near Sengstacks Road, where a millpond and falls can still be seen.

The Old Red Church: Possibly the oldest church building in the county, a sign etched over the door reads 1752, its records, written in Dutch, begin in 1766. It is the mother church of St. John's Low Dutch Reformed Church in Upper Red Hook. Services are held periodically and each Memorial Day. Losee Collection.

Martin and Zacharias Hoffman donated the land for the Old Dutch Church, which still stands on Route 9G in Tivoli. It is claimed to be the oldest church building in Dutchess County. Over the door of the old red clapboard building is the date, 1752. However, this may have been added later. The church was consecrated October 5, 1766, and Dutch records begin at that time for the "Red Church near Madalin." The brothers were the first pew holders, and Martin became a Deacon there. Madalin, a settlement one-quarter mile up the hill from Hoffman's ferry landing at the river, was considered a separate village from the landing until 1872, when the two hamlets merged and were incorporated into the Village of Tivoli. Old-timers still refer to Tivoli at the four corners as "Madalin." About 1760 Zacharias Hoffman built a large stone house on the White Clay Kill near the family's mills. It was known as "Hoffman's Castle," and survived into the 20th Century. In 1775 he and his nephews, Nicholas, Martin and Zacharias were among the signers of the "Pledge of the People of Rhinebeck," repudiating the British government. Franklin Delano Roosevelt was a direct descendent of Colonel Martin Hoffman.

"To the Width of Four Horses:" The Hamlets Along the Road

The construction of an overland road several miles east of the river gave rise to settlement of farms and hamlets inland. In 1710 the English Governor ordered the Queen Anne's Highway (known after Queen Anne's reign as the King's Highway) to be built "to a width of four horses." It came to be known as the Post Road (Route 9), and it would become the main land route connecting New York and Albany for the next 240 years. Distinctive red sandstone markers were erected noting the distance from Fort George, the seat of government of the Province at the Battery on Manhattan. Red Hook's eight markers ranged from 101 to 109. The Post Road would greatly affect the development of the town. Dutch families like the Heermances at West Kerley's Corners Road, and the Martins in the Village of Red Hook, were drawn to construct their homes near the highway. It allowed them to transport and sell their goods to local towns along the Post Road, from Kinderhook and Hudson in the north in Columbia County, to Rhinebeck and Poughkeepsie to the south. Stagecoaches transported passengers from New York to Albany, beginning in the 1750s, bringing business to innkeepers along the way. The hamlets of Upper Red Hook and the Village of Red Hook, or the "lower village," as it was called well into the 20th century, grew up along the Post Road.

Upper Red Hook c. 1890: The Post Road, or the old King's Highway, was the main route from Albany to New York. It ran through Upper Red Hook, which in the 18th and early 19th centuries was a major hamlet. The triangle still remains where the Post Road merged with Spring Lake Road, as seen in this winter scene. Losee Collection.

Upper Red Hook

Upper Red Hook got its name, not because of the relationship of the village to Red Hook Village three miles to the south (the settlement, that eventually became the largest and most active of the villages in the 20th century), but because of its position relative to the Red Hook Landing, or, Tivoli. Tivoli landing was Red Hook; the village on the upland three miles in from the river was considered Upper Red Hook.

The "village by the road," as it was sometimes called, grew up at the corner of the Post Road and several roads leading east to New England. The Heermances built their stone house near the hamlet on West Kerley's Corners Road, and the Pitchers, just a mile away, on what is today Pitcher Lane. Sometime before 1788 a new congregation of Dutch Reformed was organized to accommodate the growing population there, leaving the Old Red Church to serve those near Tivoli.

St. John's Low Dutch Reformed Church: The Reverend K.P.S. Myers stands before his 100-year-old church in Upper Red Hook in 1874. The tall graceful steeple was removed in 1963 after it had deteriorated, and replaced with a smaller one. Note the split rail fence, which lined the Post Road. Photo by Lester P. Donerly, St. John's Collection.

The "new church," called St. John's Low Dutch Reformed Church, was built in 1793 and remained affiliated with the Tivoli church. It was built of local stone quarried from the "Styler Barrick," Dutch for the rocky hill just northeast of the church. On the same hill runs Starr Barrack Road, a reminder of this original Dutch community. The Dominie who served St. John's also served the Red Church. The congregation of the reformed churches was a mix of Dutch and German ancestry. By 1806, "low Dutch," a Dutch vernacular spoken by most of the early colonists, was falling out of favor, while more and more families used English as their first language. Petrus DeWitt served the church from about 1788 to 1798, preaching in Dutch. A condition of employment for the next Dominie at St. John's and Tivoli's was, however, "to preach in such language as the consistory of the two congregations shall point out."[8]

The present church along the Post Road was built in 1871. At the time of construction, it featured a tall, graceful steeple with fine detail, but the steeple was replaced with a smaller, plain steeple in 1963. David Van Ness, an elder of the church, and the first supervisor of the Town of Red Hook, first contemplated his "blue mountains" from his house in Upper Red Hook, where he built a fine brick home, later called the Punderson House, before the Revolution. He kept a store there until around 1790. He and his wife, Cornelia Heermance, who had been born at the nearby family farm, raised 10 children.

There was an inn, a blacksmith shop, a store and several substantial houses at the crossroads in the mid-1700s. By the late 1800s, nearly 200 people supported a church, post office, school, a second tavern, a harness shop and a carriage and wagon maker. The Thomas House, a very old brick tavern, stood at the crossroads in 1777, where it was used briefly as the headquarters of Major General Israel Putnam in the Revolutionary War. It was from the Thomas House that Putnam commanded his troops in tracking the British as they came across from Kingston to menace the population of Red Hook. Mills and storehouses were burned at Barrytown and Tivoli, and the Livingston home at Clermont was destroyed, but no human casualties of the war on Red Hook soil are recorded.

The First Mills

The first mills, run by waterpower from the Saw Kill and the White Clay Kill, ground cornmeal from corn and flour from wheat. They sawed lumber from cut timber, carded wool for spinning into cloth. Fulling mills produced cloth for clothing. They were vitally important to the early settlers, who produced all the goods and food, with the exception of some items like coffee, tea and sugar, that were necessary to feed, clothe and sustain their families in this relatively untamed place. The first roads in town cut through the woods to the mills and the landings.

Site of the earliest mill: The fastest flowing section of the Saw Kill stream, which altogether supported over a half dozen mills in the 18th and 19th century, was at the two falls on the eastern stretch near Rock City. Located near Camp Rising Sun on Oriole Mills Road, the dramatic falls supported a mill there before 1769. Losee Collection.

The Chancellor's Mill: Listed on the 1797 Thompson Map, the three-story mill and millpond on Mill Road was later called Red Hook Mills. It operated, grinding corn and wheat, grain and feed, and later cutting tobacco for the local Red Hook Tobacco Company, for nearly 150 years, until being torn down in the 1930s. Harriet Martin Dey Collection.

The first Red Hook tenants would probably have ground their corn and flour at Beekman's Rhinebeck mill, built about 1715, several miles to the south. By 1725, the year Schuyler completed sale of his Red Hook property, the mill rights to the western stretch of the Saw Kill, with its four falls, were held in common by Beekman, Staats and Van Benthuysen. By 1747 Henry Beekman had acquired the lower falls at the river, near the place called Cedar Hill. This hamlet on either side of the stream became known as Annandale in the 19th century, taking the name from John Bard's estate, Annandale, in the area around present-day Bard College. Beekman sold them to his son-in-law, Judge Robert Livingston of Clermont, about the same year. Although there were some farms along the River Road and Annandale Road by the 1730s, evidence of mills prior to 1770 is hard to come by. Most likely it was at Cedar Hill (Annandale), sometime before 1770, that Livingston built the first mill on the north side of the stream where it flowed into the Hudson. It is this mill that the British burned in the Revolutionary War.[9]

As she had done with her house at Clermont, Margaret Beekman Livingston, widow of Robert "the Judge," rebuilt this mill immediately. Philip Feller, the Palatine farmer who had settled the farm just a few miles south, on River Road, just over the border of the Town of Rhinebeck line (The Feller Homestead still stands), was the miller for "Mrs. Livingston's Mill." A 1797 map of Rhinebeck Precinct shows the changing pattern of ownership that continued, more or less, over the next century. Besides Margaret Livingston's grist mill, there was the Armstrong saw mill at the middle or second falls at Annandale; the "Benthuysen" grist mill is shown at Cedar Hill, just above and east of the road where it crosses the Saw Kill; and further upstream, west of Mill Road and north of the Village of Red Hook, are the Chancellor's Mills, owned by the son of Margaret Beekman Livingston.[10] These mills changed names over the years. Joseph Spurr, who emigrated from England, ran the old Benthuysen mill at the upper falls by the mid-19th century. He had a woolen carpet mill there, and his small clapboard house, built right next to the bridge, still stands. Philip Fritz, a Frenchman, operated a grist mill and a saw mill just down stream where the Armstrong mills had been. In the late 19th century these same falls provided the hydropower for the Baker's Chocolate Factory.

Rhinebeck Map of 1797: Mapping for the Town of Rhinebeck, which included Red Hook at the time, was prepared in the months of December 1797 through January 1798 by Alexander Thompson. Mills, major houses, churches and inns that stood along main streams and roads, are shown. Delafield Collection, Princeton Universary Library, Princeton, N.J.

On the eastern reaches of the Saw Kill near Rock City, a hamlet on the border of the Red Hook/Rhinebeck precinct, there stands the remains of one of the earliest mill complexes, Oriole Mills. A long series of falls supported a large operation consisting of a fulling mill, a gristmill and a sawmill. Robert G. Livingston built a mill there, probably a grist, before 1769. This according to Helen Wilkensen Reynolds a noted county historian who wrote in the early 20th century. This then would make Oriole Mills the first mill operation in the town of Red Hook. Further to the west, the remains of one of two more Saw Kill mills still stands on Saw Mill Road. There were at least eight mill sites and water falls on the Saw Kill.

The Five Settlements

In contrast to Upper Red Hook, the lower village was a quiet backwater referred to as "Hardscrabble" in the 18th century. A hardscrabble was a place of little importance and even less prosperity. The Elmendorph Inn was built there around 1750, and there were a few farms at the corners. Two of the first settlers in Red Hook, Nicholas Bonastale (Bonesteel) and his wife Anna Margaretha Kuhns (Coons), were among the people taxed in the North Ward (Rhinebeck/Red Hook Precinct) in 1723. They were believed to have held a life lease for a farm on the south side of Barrytown Road (Route 199 west of the Village of Red Hook).[11] The Bonastale family also owned a farm near the Elmendorph.

Although the northern most settlements—Hoffman's Mills near the river and

Subdivision Map c. 1795: Showing a portion of a Bonastale (Bonesteel) family farm (12 acres) and possibly the Martin farm (2 acres), sold to Cornelius Elmendorph, who in 1799 built the Red Hook Hotel. The graphics showing the Elmendorph Inn, run at the time by Cornelius' brother John, in relation to the old Calvinist Lutheran Church (now St. Paul's) bear no resemblance to their current locations. It may be either a distortion or a mistake. Rokeby Collection.

Upper Red Hook at the Post Road—were the more active villages in the 18th century, by the time of the Revolution, settlements had also been established at Annandale (Cedar Hill) and Barrytown (Lower Landing), as well as in the Lower Village (Hardscrabble).

New York Province had already been divided into 12 counties in 1683, with the deep glens and forests along this part of the Hudson being named Dutchess after the wife of the duke of York, the governor of the province and the future King James II. By 1737, the three wards of Dutchess—the Northern, Middle and Southern—had been divided into precincts. Red Hook constituted the northern part of the Rhinebeck Precinct.

In 1715, the first county census showed 445 people in the new Dutchess, including 29 "negroes and other slaves." It began to grow rapidly, especially in the northern settlements, following the arrival of the 35 Palatine families in the North Ward the same year. The first tax assessment taken in 1723 showed twice as many taxpayers in Red Hook and Rhinebeck's northern ward as in the remaining two southern wards combined. The North Ward also paid more in taxes (54 pounds, eight shillings) than either of the other two. Leasees, in which category most Palatine farmers fell at that time, as well as those who owned their farms outright, paid taxes and were counted in the assessment roles.

By 1725, the swell of Palatines had more than doubled the population to 1,085 and 43 blacks. In 1737, the Rhinebeck Precinct recorded 3,680 inhabitants, and 262 of them black. A good half of these individuals inhabited Red Hook. As the population grew, the need for order arose.

Red Hook/Rhinebeck Precinct Established: Early Rules of the Road

The first town records for the Precinct of Rhinebeck, which included Red Hook, appeared in 1748.

Post Road, Upper Red Hook: Built in 1710, the old King's Highway, shown in this early 20th century photo, was the main road through town. The poles are probably for telegraph transmission. The Post Road was not paved until after World War I. State Route 9, bypassing the hamlet, was built in 1929. Losee Collection.

The first officials elected were the overseers of the highways and pathmasters. Maintaining the roads between farms and river landings was paramount in the early years of the town. Besides the primary north/south Post Road, the "Road to Salisbury" ran east from the Barrytown "lower landing" to Connecticut and the New England colonies (State Route 199). The "road to the Northeast" ran east from Tivoli, through Upper Red Hook and out to New England (West and East Kerley's Corners roads and Spring Lake Road). River Road was the commonly traveled route along the river, between Staatsburg in the south and Tivoli in the north (State Route 9G roughly parallels it in Red Hook).

Local pathways, like Pitcher Lane and Metzger Road, got their names from the farmers who first built them in order to reach the main roads, the river or a village. Farmers along each road supplied manpower and materials to maintain them under the direction of their neighborhood pathmaster.

The first taxes were collected to care for the poor and widows, not to build up the highways, as would become common in the 20th century. "Fenceviewers" settled property disputes about gates and fences, much like the zoning officer does today.

The public tax also helped to maintain a town pound for strays. In the interest of good order, residents were required to register their cattle and pigs with a special mark. One such registered mark was recorded in 1749: "Hole through right ear the size of a six-penny piece."[12]

The ears and sometimes tails of cattle were notched in specific patterns and registered. The law forbade uncastrated cattle, swine and sheep from roaming the roads specifically during the summer months, so it can be presumed that unfenced beasts of all kinds might be encountered during certain seasons roaming along the 18th century pathways of the town.

Livestock and horses, especially, were valuable to the early farm families, and besides the new town government, farmers began to organize to protect their property. The town's oldest ongoing society, "The Red Hook Society for the Detection and Apprehension of Horsethieves," was organized in 1796 to protect what was at that time the most valuable essential possession of the farmer—the horse, an animal that could easily be stolen, transported out of the county and sold.

Timothy Meadow, Red Hook: The horse was the farmer's most important asset, from the 18th to the mid-20th century. Horses and livestock were used to harvest crops and transport hay, grain and produce, as in this photo taken at the Lown farm in Upper Red Hook around 1920. The Society for the Prevention and Apprehension of Horsethieves protected local farmers' investments in their horses. Losee Collection.

Chapter 4
Slavery in Red Hook

from the beginning of the 18th century through the 19th century, landowners and tenants, if they were relatively prosperous, might own slaves. Slaves were considered a commodity, along with a farmer's horse and livestock, and their possession was a measure of the prosperity of a farmer or merchant. Successful tenant farmers, including Palatines, would sometimes have one or two slaves. Mohr and Heermance were listed as having several slaves each in 1755, while Colonel Martin Hoffman, the wealthy Tivoli landowner, owned 10.

As early as 1714, Robert Livingston wrote from New York to his wife, Alida, at the manor just north of Red Hook, that he was trying to find two slaves to send up to some tenants who requested he buy them. He complained that he had a hard time finding any "worth a skuiver." But after finding two, he wrote, glowingly, "They are such beautiful negroes as I have ever seen. And do not sell them for less than 50 pounds please, for they are worth it. One, the oldest, speaks English well, has been a shepherd and has been born at Jamaica. The other has first come from his land and knows nothing but (the) negro language."[13]

In Howard Morse's *1908 History of Rhinebeck*, the slave census of 1755, taken a good 40 years after the Palatines had arrived in Rhinebeck, showed a number of Red Hook Palatine families—Feller, Stickel, Benner, Soefeldt, and Ostrander—listed as slave holders, alongside the presumably more firmly established Dutch settlers. There were 52 slaveholders, owning a total of 116 slaves. Most lived and worked on small farms and slept in an attic or basement of the farmer's house, or in an outbuilding.

By the first U.S. and New York State census in 1790, there were 421 slaves listed in the precinct, out of a population of 3,755 people, with Henry G. Livingston of Tivoli in Red Hook having the most, at 13. Andries Heermance of Upper Red Hook owned 11, attesting, perhaps, to 50 years of relative prosperity for his family at the West Kerley's Corners property. Almost half of the 1,856 African American slaves counted in 1790 in the county were in white homes with three or fewer people.[14]

Following the Revolution, the movement toward manumission of slaves became stronger. However, the laws that finally passed in 1799 to begin to free slaves only chipped away at the institution. In 1820, there were still 720 slaves in Dutchess County. In 1821, a law was passed requiring the freeing of all slaves born before July 4, 1799. In essence this assured enslavement of black Americans until 1826 in New York.

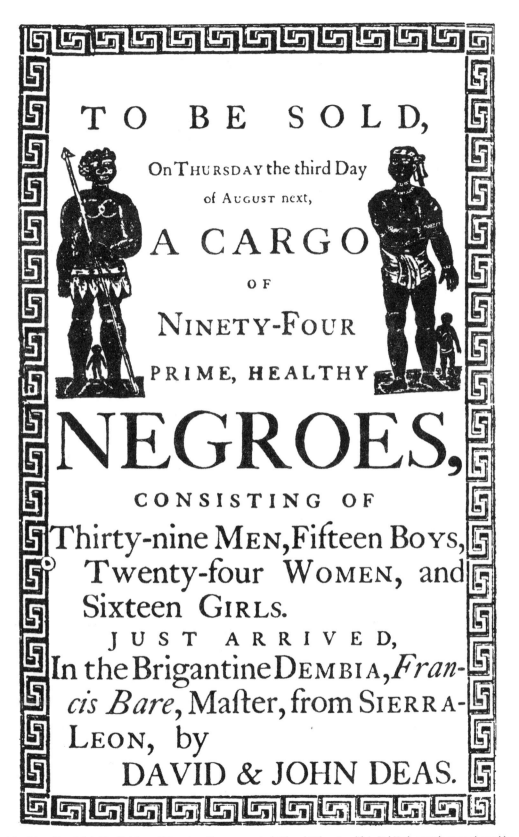

Advertising a Slave Sale in New York State, 18th century: Slaves were part of 18th and 19th century life in Red Hook, not only among the wealthy landowners, but among smaller farmers and merchants. Even some prosperous tenants owned one or two slaves to help work the farm. Graphic reprinted from Dutchess County Historical Society Yearbook, Vol. 69, 1984.

Chapter 5
The American Revolution: "Under New Men and Measures"

In April 1775, with the impending war with England at their doorstep, the men of Red Hook were asked to sign a patriot pledge repudiating the British government and placing themselves "under the power of new men and new measures." Andries Heermance of the stone house on West Kerley's Corners, and Christian More, descendant of Philip Mohr at Barrytown, signed their names right beneath local merchants and statesmen such as David Van Ness and Egbert Benson.

Egbert Benson, for whom the local historical society is named, was a prominent figure in the Revolutionary War, not as a soldier, but as a statesman. Benson was a leader of the local Committee for Safety, and it was he who was responsible for recruiting in Dutchess County. In May 1775, following the Battle of Lexington (the first clash with the British in the Revolution), the Continental Congress asked New York to recruit 10,000 soldiers. The county was at first split in its loyalty to the patriot cause. However, six months later it appeared more farmers were willing to fight for independence. By June 30, the county had filled its quota. Red Hook's old cemeteries are dotted with the graves of Revolutionary War soldiers. It was the hope of most local tenants that a successful revolution would set the tone for laws allowing them to own their land.

1790 Tombstone: Andrew P. Heermance, relative to Lieutenant Colonel Andrew Heermance, a local leader in the Revolution, is buried at St. John's Reformed Church in Upper Red Hook. There are a number of Revolutionary War soldiers buried in the churchyard, established in 1783. St. John's Reformed Church Archives.

The Breadbasket of Dutchess

By 1776, Red Hook, called the "Breadbasket of Dutchess County," was a major producer of wheat in the province. During the Revolution, about one-third of the grain and flour consumed by American troops came from Dutchess County.[15] Brigadier General James Clinton wrote to General George Washington in May of 1781, offering to send flour from the mills in Red Hook for his army. Washington approved the offer, thanking him "for obtaining bread for the Troops, in their distress, by ordering up the flour from the (Red Hook) Mills."[16] A story was told of one Red Hook man, Hendrick Weidman (Whiteman), and his son, Jacob, who had the reputation of being rebels in the Revolutionary War. They were tenant farmers who purchased the deed for their farm in Red Hook in 1796. During the winter of 1777, Jacob Whiteman delivered wheat from his Red Hook farm to the Continental army quartered at Newburgh under General Washington. He started before daybreak with sixty bushels of wheat and returned the same night, traveling seventy-six miles by horse and wagon.[17]

The Burning at Barrytown, Tivoli and Clermont

Red Hook saw action by British troops in 1777, as they traveled northward along the Hudson Valley to Albany under an ill-fated plan by British General Sir William Howe to capture New York. His plan was to split the north from the southern colonies and retake the Americas. Lieutenant General John Burgoyne was to leave from Canada to capture Albany, while Major General John Vaughan would sail up from the Hudson Highlands to take the new state capitol at Kingston, then sail north to meet Burgoyne. Vaughan broke the defensive chain placed across the river at West Point and proceeded to Kingston. His progress was shadowed on the eastern shore in Red Hook by American militia under the command of General Israel Putnam.

Clermont: *Oldest of all the Hudson River estates, Clermont was home to seven generations of Livingstons, including Margaret Beekman Livingston and her ten children, from 1730 to 1962. This house was built in 1777 on the foundations of the original, after it was burned by the British in the Revolutionary War.* Photo from A Biographical History of Clermont or Livingston Manor, Thomas Streatfeild Clarkson, Clermont, 1869. Rokeby Collection.

Based in Fishkill, Putnam made his temporary quarters at the Thomas House, an imposing brick house, which still stands in Upper Red Hook and was operated as a tavern. However Putnam, whom some historians have judged not to be a very aggressive or effective general, was not successful in stopping Vaughan from his primary assault on the rebel government in the Hudson Valley—the burning of Kingston on October 16, 1777. That night Vaughan anchored off Kingston. To add insult to injury, the next day he took a party and landed at Rhinecliff. He marched his men north, burning a warehouse at Red Hook's Lower Landing (Barrytown), Mrs. Livingston's mill at Annandale and the Hoffmans' mills at Tivoli. Proceeding upriver to their primary target, the soldiers burned Chancellor Livingston's house, as well as his mother's, at Clermont, dealing a deliberate and specific blow to that patriot family. His mother, Margaret Beekman Livingston, had her house rebuilt within a year, displaying the strong, independent temperament that led 20 years later to the development of the town.

Red Hook, October 20, 1777: Burgoyne Surrendered

If Putnam didn't save the day for the patriots, he may be credited with delivering the news of what has been called one of the ten most decisive battles in world history from the Town of Red Hook. On Oct. 7, 1777, Continental forces defeated Burgoyne's army at Saratoga, foiling the British plan to split the former colonies. However, Major General Horatio Gates, who had succeeded Major General Philip Schuyler in command of the battle, had neglected to send the news of the English surrender to his commander-in-chief. In a dispatch datelined "Red Hook, October 20, 1777," Putnam gave George Washington the first word of the

Putnam Headquarters: The former Thomas Tavern in Upper Red Hook was the temporary quarters for General Israel Putnam in 1777. Putnam monitored the actions of the British, who burned mills and grain stores along the shore before burning Clermont *and Arryl House. It is believed, however, that not a shot was fired in Red Hook.* Photo by Len Vogler.

terms of Burgoyne's capitulation. With the British defeat at Saratoga, the course of the war was turned around, and the victory of the American colonies assured.[18]

Vaughn was still anchored just north of Tivoli on October 23—"The armed vessel highest up the river lay just above the 'Lover's Leap'—a tall bluff covered with glorious evergreens—about three-quarters of a mile north of Tivoli Station. The rest were strung out southward for over two miles"—when Vaughn suddenly turned his fleet around "to the astonishment of the American patrol on shore."[19] Instead of going north to meet Burgoyne, according to plan, he quickly sailed south. The delay became apparent when the colonial world was finally officially informed of Burgoyne's defeat to the north by Putnam's Red Hook missive.

Egbert Benson

Egbert Benson: The town historical society was named after this patriot statesman and lawyer who practiced law and lived with his relatives, the Hoffmans, in Tivoli. He wrote much of New York's early law and worked for the adoption of the new federal Constitution. Portrait of Egbert Benson by Gilbert Stuart (1794). John Jay Homestead, Katonah, New York.

Egbert Benson was born in New York City in 1746, and came to Red Hook to practice law in 1772 when he was 26 years old. He graduated from Kings College and clerked for John Morin Scott, one of the leaders of the New York Bar before the Revolution. He was familiar with Red Hook. As a boy he visited his aunt, Tryntjie Benson Hoffman in Tivoli. His classmates at Kings College included Chancellor Robert Livingston of Clermont and John Jay, who became life-long friends, as did Alexander Hamilton. It is most likely that his residence was at Tivoli with the Hoffmans, during his years in Red Hook. In several letters, postmarked Red Hook, he refers to his "landlord," Mr. Hoffman, and asks his clients to address their letters to his home. In one visit to a client, Mrs. Hoffman accompanied him, since she was a friend of the family.[20]

Though his career took a very different turn, when Benson arrived in Red Hook he had every intention of staying for good, making his living here and practicing law quietly, far from the chaos and crowds of New York City. However, he had just opened his law office when the possibility of some prominent local competition gave him some pause. The future chancellor and great-grandson of the lord of Livingston Manor, young Robert R. Livingston, was rumored to be coming home to live and practice law. Benson hadn't begun to make any money (a factor that followed his career for the rest of his life) and he worried that the influential standing of young Robert's family would draw clients away from his own fledgling practice. Livingston wrote to a friend:

> *I have never been properly fixed since I came into practice... Here at least I thought myself happily settled and my prospects were as favorable as I could reasonably desire, but this sad circumstance interposing has been the cause of some uneasiness to me. However I am determined that since I am here that here I will remain while I keep soul and body together, always observing the maxim, to cut my coat according to my cloth."*[21]

He needn't have worried, because before Benson was able to settle in his Dutchess County practice, the war broke out, changing the course of his life for good. Benson became chairman of the county committee to detect conspiracies during the war, and was appointed by General George Washington to negotiate on behalf of the Army in a contracting dispute at West Point. He was elected to the first Legislative Assembly of the state in 1777, the same year he was appointed the state's first attorney general, a post he kept until 1789. He has been credited with drafting most of the new legislation passed in the first years of the Assembly. In 1788, New York drafted its first statute allowing the manumission of slaves, and in the municipal records book maintained in Poughkeepsie, where he lived when the Assembly was in session, Benson's name was the first on the list of those to free their slaves.

Benson was a zealous federalist, working to establish a strong federal government and a new U.S. Constitution. He was a delegate to the Continental Congress from 1784 until 1788. In 1786, he represented New York State at the Annapolis Convention, which recommended and resulted in the forming of the U.S. Constitution to replace the weaker Articles of Confederation, under which the first government was formed. In 1789, after working vigorously, often behind the scenes, to get the Constitution successfully adopted (New York was the 11th of 13 states to do so), he was elected one of the six representatives from New York to the first federal Congress. In 1794 he was appointed a New York State Supreme Court judge. He resigned in 1801 when appointed by President John Adams as a federal Supreme Court judge under a new arrangement of the federal circuit court system. The next term, under President Thomas Jefferson, the law creating the new federal circuit judges was repealed, and Benson and his fellow judges resigned. They became known in the history books as the "midnight judges."

Benson retired and lived 30 more years of his long life in Jamaica, Queens, traveling frequently back to the Hudson Valley. He was a bachelor and the founding president of The New-York Historical Society.

Chapter 6
Margaret Beekman Livingston Breaks Up the Beekman Patent

*t*he town got its greatest boost after the breakup of the Beekman patent. The huge landholdings in Dutchess and Ulster counties came to be owned, in an unusual 18th century twist, by a woman—Margaret Beekman Livingston. And, in an all too familiar fashion, the village was first developed "on spec" as a promising sub-division and real estate investment by two ambitious landowners.

Margaret Beekman Livingston (1724-1800): The daughter of the largest landowner in Red Hook/Rhinebeck Precinct, Margaret Beekman married Robert Livingston in December of 1742, and made Clermont her seasonal home, and home to her ten children, for the ensuing 58 years. The John Wollaston portrait of Mrs. Livingston as a young woman (left) was painted c. 1750. The Gilbert Stuart portrait (right) was painted c. 1794, and is one of four portraits of Margaret Beekman Livingston – one of which hangs at Montgomery Place—painted by Stuart, who visited Clermont in 1794. Both reprinted by permission of Clermont State Historic Site, New York State Office of Parks, Recreation and Historic Preservation.

Margaret Beekman Livingston, into whose possession the Red Hook lands fell, was the daughter of patentee Henry Beekman, one of the richest men in the region with land holdings throughout Dutchess and Ulster counties, including much of Red Hook. When he died in January 1776, she was his only heir.

Because she was a woman, her father's vast estate would ordinarily, in time, have passed directly to her husband, Robert Livingston. Upon her husband's death, the Beekman property would then have passed on to her first son, Chancellor Robert Livingston. However, her husband died in December, 1775, just two weeks before her father, leaving her a widow. Under law, Margaret inherited Beekman's entire estate. Had her husband died just after her father, instead of just before, her first son, Chancellor Robert Livingston of Clermont, would have inherited all of the Beekman lands, bypassing his mother and her heirs entirely.

Margaret Livingston was a remarkable woman. She had borne 11 children in the mid-18th century, and raised ten of them to adulthood, a remarkable feat in itself. She often managed the Clermont farm herself, since her husband and son were away regularly on other business. When the British burned her home, Margaret, then a widow, gathered her household and fled to safety overland to Connecticut in a horse and cart (but not before burying the family silver and other valuables in the yard at Clermont to protect them from the enemy). She returned the same year to rebuild her house.

Margaret Livingston and the Drawing of the Straws

Margaret was no less enterprising when it came to her vast inheritance. Rather than keep the land herself, which she could have done by law, she ordered a survey and subdivision of the estate, dividing the lands into nine shares. Then in 1783 she arranged a drawing of straws among her nine remaining heirs to distribute the Beekman landholdings. As her children spread out to manage, lease and settle on their land, which ranged north from Staatsburg to Tivoli and Clermont, they created one of the largest concentrations of grand estates in the nation.

Alida Livingston, Margaret's youngest daughter, drew the straw that gave her 8,000 acres of Red Hook land, along with 20,000 acres of the old Hardenburgh patent across the river in the Catskills (in the vicinity of the former Village of Fleishmann). The boundaries in Red Hook followed the old lines of the Schuyler/Beekman patent, running east from the river and the south side of the Saw Kill, through the lower village to the Milan town line, and south to Steen Valetje at the border of Rhinebeck. When Alida married Revolutionary War Brigadier General John Armstrong in 1789, the land became his.

Alida Livingston Armstrong and her daughter, Margaret: The Livingstons' youngest daughter drew the 7th lot in the Beekman lottery, which gave her 28,000 acres, including most of the town of Red Hook. Her daughter, Margaret, was raised at LaBergerie (Rokeby), and later married William B. Astor. Copy of a painting by Rembrandt Peale. Rokeby Collection.

The ensuing plans by Alida's husband in 1795 to develop the village may have been a reason why the upper hamlet never grew to the extent that the lower village did. That year Armstrong and his neighbor, Brigadier General David Van Ness, subdivided what amounted to over one-quarter of the present village—the northeast and southeast quadrants. A copy of the survey map is displayed in the Elmendorph Inn. Thirty-four lots between one-half and two acres were carved from a farm leased by Aaron Whiteman, south of the Elmendorph. The map outlines Cherry Street (the old Road to Salisbury), South and North Broadway (Post Road) and the newly created East Market Street. A second map dated a few years later contains the names of some of the new occupants: Martin, Moore, Lown, Van Benthuysen, Rowe, and Seimon, among them. In the margins of the old document, which was found in the attic at Rokeby, are scribbled tallies of the rents due.

Brigadier General John Armstrong: Armstrong, a major in the Continental Army and anonymous author of the controversial Newburgh Addresses, he married Alida Livingston in 1789. Thus he became landlord to much of the town, including the lower village. The 1795 survey map, a copy of which hangs in the Elmendorph Inn, shows the new lots created along Cherry Street and East Market Street, with names and tallied rents jotted along the margins. Portrait by Rembrandt Peale, U.S. National Parks Service, Philadelphia. Rokeby Collection.

Peace and Prosperity

Elmendorph Inn: The c. 1750 inn and stagecoach stop was about to be demolished to make way for a parking lot when the community stepped in to save it in 1976. It survived and has been restored through the efforts of Friends of Elmendorph and grants from the state Office of Parks, Recreation and Historic Preservation. The Elmendorph Inn is a meeting place for community groups and special events, and is home to the Egbert Benson Historical Society of Red Hook. Losee Collection.

The end of the 18th century was a time of relative peace and prosperity. The population had grown considerably and the war was over. Good wheat from Dutchess County farmers was being ground into flour in local mills, then shipped in barrels to the Caribbean, Europe and New York City. New York City, with its large markets conveniently located just a few days sail by sloop, provided a cash cow for tenant farmers and landowners alike. The hamlets were expanding into business and trade. The half dozen mills operating on the Saw Kill produced lumber, cloth, leather, flour, cornmeal, carded wool, carpet and linen. There were an additional five on the White Clay Kill, plus two river landings, three or four east/west roads, as well as the River Road and the main artery, the Albany Post Road.

The lower village, which is today the commercial center of the town, began to grow in importance. The Elmendorph Inn, which had been built at the corner of the Post Road and the Road to Salisbury sometime before 1769, was listed for sale in 1783, "an elegant house... with 80 very good apple trees... and some very good plum trees."[22]

In 1797, stages began to leave New York City on a regular basis for the trip to Albany along the Post Road. The stages left New York at 10 a.m. arriving in Albany at 9 a.m. four days later. By the late 1700s, John Elmendorph was operating the building as an inn and tavern, and one of the regular stops to board and refresh passengers and horses on the Albany-New York run became Red Hook's Elmendorph's Inn. In 1799, John's brother, Cornelius Elmendorph, built a second inn just down the road to the southwest, later to be called the Red Hook Hotel, a tavern that would not enjoy its heyday until the 1940s.

The Elmendorph became an important meeting place in the early 19th century. It was the site of the county's first agricultural fair, the first town kindergarten, and it hosted the first Red Hook town meetings in 1815.

By the early 1800s, Lower Red Hook had grown sufficiently to warrant its own organizations, separate from Upper Red Hook, and it was at the Elmendorph that the Independent Horse Thieves Society of the Lower Village was formed in 1827. The inn deteriorated in the 19th century and was literally spared from the jaws of a bulldozer near the end of the 20th.

The town was beginning to grow. In the Rhinebeck/Red Hook precinct, there were 514 heads of families, 875 white males over 16 and 2,300 women and children in 1790, compared to 80 heads of household 50 years earlier in 1740. The tax assessment roll of 1799 showed the majority of the 525 heads of household in the greater Rhinebeck/Red Hook Precinct were of German and Dutch descent. Most of these, including some Palatine names, were listed as having "house and barns," valued between $1,000 and $3,000, assessed at between $1 and $3 a year.[23] These were farmers such as Mohr in Barrytown, the Martins in the Village of Red Hook, and the Heermances in Upper Red Hook, who owned the simple but substantial one-and-one-half-story farmhouses that can still be seen today.

View of the Cookingham Farm, 19th Century: The original Gotlieb Martin farm in the Village of Red Hook remains a working farm today. In the 19th century, this was a typical landscape in villages and countryside. Fred Briggs Collection.

Chapter 7
Fancy Acres and the Era of the Great Estates

*t*he breakup of the huge Beekman/Livingston landholdings among the heirs of Margaret Beekman Livingston heralded the era of the Great Hudson River Estates —a phenomena that continues to define the town's unique riverfront landscape.

View from Montgomery Place: *Alexander Jackson Davis made extensive renovations to Janet Montgomery's house in the 1840s, although the estate has remained a working farm throughout its transformations. The woodcut made from this Davis sketch is from Andrew Jackson Downing's "The Horticulturist, and Journal of Rural Art and Rural Taste." From "Sketches of Montgomery Place" by A.J. Davis, Historic Hudson Valley, 1988.*

Between 1790 and 1940, the ten Livingston children and their kin built more than three dozen grand houses overlooking the Hudson River. These country seats, as they came to be called, stretched south from Olana in Columbia County, to Staatsburg. Over one dozen houses were built along Red Hook's shoreline.

The estates were conceived when the early landowners first noticed the beautiful vistas of the farms that they leased out by the river, with their views of the Hudson and the Catskills beyond. They began to trade their inland property for the riverside farms leased by their tenants. Henry Beekman and Robert Livingston started this trend in the 18th century, but it wasn't until the early 19th century that the process accelerated. The local farmer was frequently the beneficiary in this tendency of the wealthy toward "fancy acres," or land that that was pretty, but not necessarily practical. The riverside was composed of clay, and the interior lands in Red Hook contained some of the finest farmland in the state—as it does to this day. As the 19th century essayist Nathaniel Parker Willis observed, the times were producing "a class who could afford to let the trees grow." This was a development few canny farmers could resist.

Willis related the story of a Hudson Valley man who met his neighbor one day, piled atop a horse and cart, setting off with his entire household:

> *He was going twenty miles farther back, where a man could afford to farm, at the price of the land. His cornfields on the banks of the Hudson had risen in value, as probable sites for ornamental residences, and with the difference (between $200 the fancy acre, and $60 the farming acre) in his pocket... he was four or five thousand dollars richer in capital, and only a loser in scenery.*[24]

In a typical trade, Valentine Bender (Benner), a Palatine who leased 151 acres in Barrytown from Henry Beekman, moved two miles east after exchanging his riverside farm for his landlord's inland acres.[25] A road still bears his name west of Red Hook Village, where he settled and established quite a prosperous farm, despite his lack of a view.

In Red Hook, the Hudson shoreline was almost entirely taken up by Margaret's children, all of whom were the beneficiaries of the straw lottery. They built their houses, as their parents had done, overlooking the river. *Belvedere,* and later

Arryl House, *or* New Clermont, *was built by Chancellor Robert Livingston in 1794, just a stone's throw south of his mother's* Clermont, *at the time a part of Red Hook and the Greater Rhinebeck township. The Chancellor died there in 1813. The house burned in 1909, leaving the picturesque ruins we see today.* Rokeby Collection.

Arryl House, were built by the oldest son, the Chancellor, right next door to his mother's house, *Clermont.* The foundations of *Arryl House* still stand. *Montgomery Place* was built by the oldest daughter, Janet Livingston Montgomery, in 1805, 30 years after she and her husband, General Richard Montgomery, built *Grasmere* in Rhinebeck. *Massena,* in the hamlet of Barrytown, was built by John R. Livingston; and *LaBergerie,* later named *Rokeby,* was built by Alida Livingston and her husband, General John Armstrong.

Armstrong served as a U.S. senator, minister to France and secretary of war during the War of 1812. Serious about improving agriculture in the region and making his own farm profitable, he published a widely read treatise on the subject that was printed in three editions during a 40-year period. *Rokeby* became the home of the celebrated Astor family after Armstrong's daughter married William Backhouse Astor, son of John Jacob Astor. After Janet's death, *Montgomery Place* was inherited by Edward Livingston, the youngest child. A former mayor of New York City, Edward Livingston served in Congress from Louisiana, and became U.S. secretary of state and minister to France. He returned to Red Hook in 1835 to retire and pursue a life of agriculture. However, he died just one year later.

LaBergerie: *The home of John and Alida Armstrong at Barrytown,* LaBergerie *was sold to their daughter, Margaret and her husband William B. Astor, who renamed it* Rokeby *and later, extensively altered the house, adding, among other features, an octagonal tower with an extensive library. The house has remained in the same family for nearly 200 years.* Rokeby Collection.

Original Massena: *Built by John R. Livingston in 1797, this early photo shows the elegance of the house that was reknowned as being one of the most beautiful places in the valley. Among its special features was a prized library with a soaring, glass-domed ceiling. The building burned and was rebuilt and is now on the campus of the Unification Church Theological Seminary.* Rokeby Collection.

Livingston kin—uncles, cousins and in-laws—built more houses along the river. *Callendar House* and *The Pynes* were built in Tivoli before 1800. By 1905, six more estates had risen above the Red Hook shoreline: *Rose Hill* and *Teviot* in Tivoli; *Edgewater, Sylvania* and *Steen Valetje* in Barrytown; and *Blithewood* in Annandale. All of these houses survive, and several of them still remain in the original families. Others, the original *Massena,* the *Cruger House, Miramonte* (formerly the old Van Benthuysen house), *Almont* (formerly *De Veaux Park* and now the site of *Ward Manor* at Bard College). *Parndon* and the *Chateau de Tivoli,* have been gone for a century or more.

Edgewater: *This classic Greek Revival house, set at the water's edge at Barrytown, was built in 1820 by John R. Livingston for his daughter Margaretta Livingston Brown. When the new railroad was constructed, passing her east windows by just a few yards and bringing with it noise and soot, the then widowed Mrs. Brown sold the house to Robert Donaldson and fled in indignation to Europe. She never returned. Donaldson commissioned A.J. Davis in 1853 to design several buildings and a magnificent octagonal library. In the 1950s, author Gore Vidal lived there. It is now owned by Richard Jenrette, who has renovated and restored the house and grounds.* Photo by Tom Daley.

Gathering for a circus at Ward Manor c. 1929: *Established on the site of one of the earliest Livingston houses, John Armstrong's The Meadows, this 1000-acre estate has been called, under various owners,* DeVeaux Park, Almont *(R.S. Livingston), and the* Hamersley place. *The house was built about 1915 and sold to the Ward Baking Company in 1926. The estate was transformed by philanthropist William Matthews into the* Ward Manor *community, pictured here, a place of recuperation for working and low-income families from New York City. In the 1960s, targeted as a site for a nuclear power plant, it was bought by the state Department of Environmental Conservation. The house was deeded to Bard College, as a dormitory. The land is now a state wildlife reserve.* Donna Matthews Collection.

It was the custom of these families to spend summers on the river, where they would escape from the heat and unhealthy conditions of the city. They would then return for the winter "season" of theater, concerts and parties to their homes in New York City, where many of the men had business interests. This became especially so in the mid-19th century.

In the Town of Red Hook, the "great houses," and the American story with which they are intricately connected, remain uniquely important. For while the huge landholdings blocked access to the river in a way that limited opportunities for growth for less wealthy citizens, their proprietors ultimately enabled the preservation of most of the magnificent shoreline of the upper Hudson. Through the popular public preservation movement in the last half of the 20th century, the landscape and architecture of this period—including the Great Houses and Red Hook hamlets that comprise their country settings—were designated by the U.S. Secretary of the Interior, in 1990, as one of the largest landmark districts in the nation. The Hudson River National Historic Landmark District extends from Germantown to Hyde Park and includes the entire Red Hook shoreline area and three of the town's five villages and hamlets.

Callendar House: *Built at Tivoli by Henry Gilbert Livingston in 1794, this grand Federal-style house overlooking the Hudson in Tivoli, was first called* Sunning Hill. *It was the home of the Redmond family in the 20th century. Part of the old farm now serves as the Kaatsbaan Dance Center.* Photo by Tom Daley.

Rose Hill: *J.W. DePeyster completed this villa in Tivoli in 1860. It became the Leake and Watts Orphanage and farm in 1908. In 1953 it was bought as a retreat for Catholic Workers by Dorothy Day, the 20th century pacifist and advocate for the poor, who is being considered for canonization.* Photo by Tom Daley.

The story of some of Red Hook's Great Houses and the families that owned them has been told in detail in several publications.

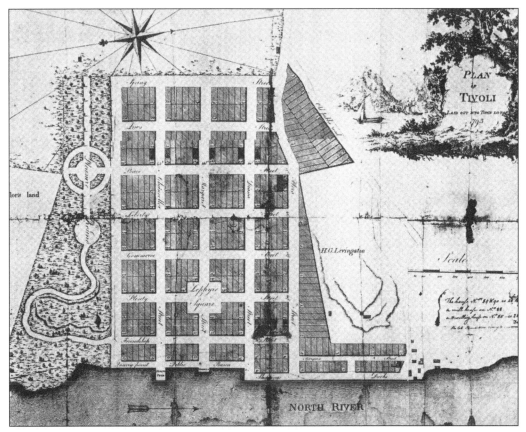

De Labigarre's Tivoli: Peter de Labigarre, a French immigrant whose estate gave the Village of Tivoli its name, has long gone, as has his Chateau de Tivoli. But certain street names in the village remain as evidence of his grand, but unfinished, plan to design and build the ideal community in this northern Red Hook village. De Labigarre commissioned Charles de Saint-Memin, a French portrait painter and engraver, to design and produce a copper engraving of the planned community, which shows the pattern of streets laid out neatly around a central square. The streets bore names such as Zephyr Square, Diana, Peace and Plenty. There was Liberty Street and Chancellor Street, in a nod to his friend Robert R. Livingston, and Commerce Street, in a bid for prosperity. De Labigarre went bankrupt before he could complete his plans, and Flora and Friendship streets, as well as Tivoli's distinctive name, are all that remain of his visionary scheme. Taken from "Orders from France" by Roger G. Kennedy.

Chapter 8
Red Hook Splits from Rhinebeck

While the estates began to go up along the river, life in the town continued to flourish. The population in Rhinebeck precinct grew from 3,755 in 1790 to 4,485 in 1810. It was growing so well that the town, held to its ancient boundaries, was becoming too populous to be governed responsively.

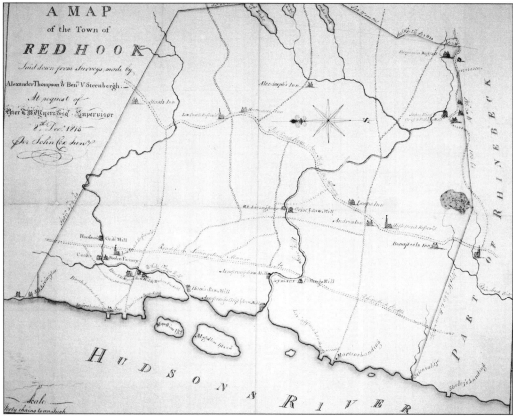

First Red Hook Map: Commisioned in 1815, just after the Red Hook/Rhinebeck split, this Thompson/Van Steenburgh map shows the mills, river landings (two each at Barrytown and Tivoli) and the major inns, including Loops (Elmemdorph Inn) and Andrus (the Red Hook Hotel razed in 1963) in the village. EBHSRH Archives.

The growth, beginning in the late 1700s, was part of an economic boom in the Northeast. By now, there were more roads, more markets and more opportunities to purchase or lease land. The demand for wheat was growing in New England, Europe and the Caribbean following the outbreak of the French Revolution, and in burgeoning New York City just 100 miles away. In Red Hook, wheat was the primary crop, averaging 10 bushels an acre, sometimes averaging as high as 16. The harvest was brought to local mills to be ground into flour. Oxen- or horse-drawn carts carried what was not used at home to the landings at Tivoli or Barrytown. From there, sloops and barges carried the precious commodity to market. The Hudson River remained the most important means of commercial transportation. In 1807, following earlier experiments with steam navigation in the North Bay near Tivoli, and with the encouragement of his wife's cousin and guardian, Chancellor Livingston, Robert Fulton built and operated the world's first commercially successful steamboat. The *North River* was later informally known as *The Clermont,* in honor of his patron. But it would not be until mid-century that the steamboat, along with the influence of the railroad and the Erie Canal, would spell the decline of sloops on the Hudson.

Sheep were the most important livestock. Large operations were established near Barrytown at La Bergerie, Montgomery Place and Massena. Their wool fostered secondary industries in finishing the woven cloth. Flax was grown for the production of linen cloth and cotton was imported from the south for muslin cloth. Carding mills and woolen mills finished the wool, which was spun by women at home. In 1813, 16,000 yards of cloth were woven in Red Hook households by women.[26]

Sheep at Massena c. 1890: Massena's *large herd of Merino sheep was one of number of herds established at farms and estates in 19th century Red Hook.* Rokeby Collection.

Transportation was by foot, if you were not lucky enough to have a horse. In 1812, getting to a town meeting in Rhinebeck meant an hour-long horseback ride along eight miles of the River Road or the Post Road from Red Hook. Farmers had the further advantage of a wagon. However, you could always catch a ride by stagecoach in Upper Red Hook or at Elmendorph's in the lower village. These daily stage stops for travelers between New York and Albany had been established in 1797.

As the population of the old Rhinebeck Precinct approached 5,000, state senator Morgan Lewis of Staatsburg introduced a bill partitioning the town. The split took affect on April 6, 1813.

The first Red Hook town meeting was held that month at the inn of Henry Walter, later called the Red Hook Hotel. Citizens elected the 71-year old merchant and Revolutionary War soldier, David Van Ness, to be the town's first supervisor. They elected overseers of the roads and of the poor, a tax collector, three constables, a poundmaster and six fenceviewers, the fore-runners of today's zoning enforcement officers. Fenceviewers were paid six shillings for their time in policing fences, settling boundary disputes and seeing that neighbors bore repair costs equally. Taxes were levied for the primary purpose of taking care of the poor and widowed. Penalties collected from violating the town code were also to be distributed to the poor. In 1812, the precinct had collected and spent $1,750 on their care.

Henry Walter's Inn: Later known as the Red Hook Hotel, the 1799 inn built in the center of Red Hook Village by Cornelius Elmendorph at the corner of the Post Road (Route 9) and the road to the Lower Landing (Barrytown) was the scene of the first town meeting, when Red Hook split from Rhinebeck in 1813. Losee Collection.

No Male Swine Allowed

The new pound master was Nicholas Hoffman Jr. and he had more to contend with in the new town than dogs. The following entry appears in the town's first record book:

"Resolved… that all swine running at large shall be sufficiently run and yoked….

"…That no boar or male swine shall be permitted to run at large (between April 1st and December 1st)… if found. Any person shall have the right to castrate the same at the risk of the owner or put such boar into the public pound."

The same fate awaited unpenned rams. Among the other laws passed that day: Fences must be four-and-one-half feet high and the owners of cattle running loose would be fined $5 a "creature." Costs of repair and upkeep of roads were to be borne by neighborhood farmers, who volunteered their labor to maintain roads and build bridges under the direction of the overseer (it was not until 1900, that highway maintenance, now the bulk of the municipal budget, was switched to a money-based, rather than labor-based system). Among the state mandates adopted that day by the new town was a duty to control all wolves, bears and panthers, "and for the destruction of the noxious weed, Canada Thistle."[27]

Red Hook's First Supervisor

Maizefield: *When he moved from Upper Red Hook to the lower village around 1795, David Van Ness built his house with a commanding western view, "beneath the blue mountains," as he ever after referred to his home. With its fine Palladian window and geometric motifs, the Georgian-Federal house is considered one of the finest examples of post-Revolutionary war construction.* Photo by Douglas Baz.

When he was elected supervisor in 1813, David Van Ness had lived in Red Hook for 45 years. He had raised 10 children in Upper Red Hook, served on the consistory of St. John's Low Dutch Reformed Church, and was president of the Horse Thieves association. Besides investing with John Armstrong to develop the lower village, he had a number of business interests, including a slate quarry operation near Rhinebeck. He twice served as supervisor of the Precinct of Rhinebeck.

As a young man, he served as a captain in the Continental Army; then as a major in a regiment of Dutchess Militia. After the war, he rose in rank. Between 1793 and 1801, he held a commission as general of a Brigade. Although he characterized himself as "merchant" in early censuses, he was always referred to locally as "general."

Van Ness built his beautiful Federal-style brick house, Maizefield, near the main east-west road to Red Hook landing. He had served for years as Red Hook postmaster. When he moved to lower Red Hook village and built his new house in 1799, he moved the town's post office and village name along with him. Van Ness would serve only one year of his new post, before moving to Troy in 1814, where he died in 1818.

A young man, A. Eggleston, writing from Tivoli in 1815, allows us a glimpse of the privilege, beauty and, apparently, the roughness that coincided in Red Hook life at the turn of the 19th century. He had just started a job as tutor to two Livingston families, dividing his time between Chancellor Robert Livingston's three children at Clermont, and Philip Livingston's four at Callendar House. He wrote to his friend, asking him to help arrange for some books to be sent, telling a little about his new situation:

> *Mr. R. Livingston lives in Clermont and P.H. Livingston in Redhook about two miles distant. I board in Redhook (Tivoli) between them & attend to each family three hours in a day... My task is light One only of the whole contemplates studying latin soon, though he has not commenced yet. I have a pleasant walk on the banks of the river of two miles between the Livingstons. In severe storms, however, it will be rather more disagreable: but in warm pleasant weather it is almost the whole distance, completely shaded.... The neighborhood in which I reside is an abandoned place. I have heard more swearing and seen more drunkenness within the space of less than one week that I have been here, than I have heard and seen within a whole year past.*
>
> *Yours&c*
> *A. Eggleston* [28]

Chapter 9
The Nineteenth Century

With the birth of the new town came the beginnings of dramatic change in the 19th century. The old horse-powered ferries, which had replaced the earlier boats and scows at the Hudson River crossing at Tivoli, were in turn replaced by steam ferries. Steamboats, introduced in 1807, eventually replaced the graceful Hudson River sloops that had brought wheat to the New York troops during the Revolution. By the 1840s, day and night steamers stopped regularly at Tivoli and Barrytown to pick up passengers and produce, and drop off mail on their regular New York-Albany run. The steamboats were faster than the sloops, which took as many as 10–12 days to complete the round trip to New York. The Central Hudson Steamboat Company, running boats from Newburgh to Albany in the 1870s, left Newburgh at 7 a.m., taking four-and-one-half-hours to reach Barrytown and five hours to Tivoli.[29]

In the 1830s, the area's wheat market softened considerably when the Erie and the smaller Delaware and Hudson (D&H) canals opened up competitive markets and cheaper flour poured out of western New York and the upper Midwest via the Great Lakes. The Dutchess Breadbasket disappeared. Red Hook farmers began to diversify, turning to dairy, livestock and fruit production for profit—perishable products for which their proximity to New York City gave them an edge.

Fulton & Best Ad: *The freighting firm at Barrytown advertised their 1860 season in the* Red Hook Journal, *preparing to run the barge,* Mayflower, *between Barrytown and New York as soon as the ice broke.* Maynard Ham Collection.

Pork, hay, buckwheat and apples were now sent to market from Barrytown and Tivoli, with farmers coming from as far away as Connecticut to ship their produce down the river to New York. In one of Red Hook's earliest manufacturing efforts, the production of cigars and snuff, the raw material, tobacco, made its way to the Red Hook factory via the river.

The very same year Red Hook became an independent town, new state laws mandated that each community set up a public school system. The new system joined an earlier push for education in Red Hook among small, subscription schools.

The First of the "One-Room" Schoolhouses

The first Red Hook public schools were organized in 1813. Eventually nine schools were built near the most populated neighborhoods. Some of them took the place of small, private subscription schools that were run in homes or central locations. One early school was taught in the small house west of today's Key Bank in the village. It is now a restaurant. An attempt was made to locate schoolhouses so that no six-year old child would have to walk more than four miles round trip in bad weather—the big yellow bus was a century in to the future.

Cokertown Schoolhouse: Students of all ages walked to their local one- and two-room schools, like this one on the eastern border of town on Jackson Corners Road. While the teacher taught the youngest, the oldest studied their lessons until it was their turn. Will Teator Collection.

Red Hook Academy: This subscription school was built in 1822 by Philip Clum of Clermont, the builder of the Clermont Academy, and bore a striking resemblance to that historic building. When it burned in 1917, his grandson Philip rebuilt it. By 1900 it served as the Red Hook Grange. Losee Collection.

The Elmendorph School was the first public school organized in Red Hook. Located at the corner of Budd's Corners and Whalesback roads near the Elmendorph Farm, it served students from outlying areas as well during its early years. Its early school board rules are typical of the way most of the nine schools were set up: The families were expected to contribute firewood for each child, "cut short for the stove." On the day set for delivery, "taxpayers who have no wood, will attend with their axes and help cut wood."[30]

The first school costs were listed in pounds and pence: pail and mug, 5/2; nails, l/9; boards, 15/; to carpenter for laying floor, one pound sterling." The 1815 accounting is some indication of when the first Elmendorph School was built. In 1855, $155 was raised to replace it.[31]

The Red Hook Academy

Among the small private schools in town, The Red Hook Academy, which was run as a boarding and subscription school for more than 35 years, was exceptional.

Fraleigh School Children, 1911: School District #5, the Fraleigh School, was located on the banks of the Saw Kill adjacent to the farm of the late Irving Fraleigh on the Road to Rock City (Route 199). In 1824, $100 was spent to hire a teacher for 66 pupils, grades one through twelve, enrolled that year. It is now a private home. Mary Willets Collection.

It was established in Upper Red Hook in 1822 by a group of families encouraged by the local minister from St. John's Dutch Reformed Church, the Reverend Andrew N. Kittle. John S. and Henry Livingston put up one-third of the $1,210 needed to build the school. Prosperous farm families like the Fraleighs and the Pitchers came up with the rest.

The first year, 45 students attended, their families paying four to six dollars for a boy, and three to five dollars for a girl, for each eleven-week quarter. If you came from out of town, it cost $50 to board at the home of the teacher, who was also the principal.

The Academy developed an excellent reputation and drew students from Albany to New York City. The punishable offenses set down in the 1823 book of student duties were typical of the early private schools:

Students will be punctual... all profane or vulgar language or immoral conduct is to be checked... all students are expected to attend public worship on the Sabbath at their regular place of worship... students shall not frequent stores except when they have business that makes it necessary to be there.[32]

In 1858 the Academy became a parochial school for St. John's Dutch Reformed Church. A few years after that it housed another private school, Mountain View Academy. By 1900, it was being used as a grange hall and community center until it burned to the ground in 1917 after being struck by lightening. It was rebuilt, but contrary to the old saying that lightening never strikes twice, it did, the second time in 1954. That time it was not rebuilt.

In 1842, when the state passed laws disallowing landholdings granted by charters and renewed by letters patent (the old manorial system that had given rise to the system of large estates and tenant farms), there was an immediate increase in population and enterprise in the town. Between 1840 and 1860, the population shot up by more than one-third from 2,833 to 3,755, and Red Hook experienced a commercial and residential building boom.

The Curtis House: John Curtis sold stoves, peddled his tinware out in the countryside in a horse and wagon and installed many of the tin roofs that are still to be seen in the village. He raised his family in this house on West Market Street, now site of the Key Bank. Losee Collection.

The Curtis Hardware Store: John Curtis sold his stoves from this store, which he ran with his brother LeGrand in the 1850s. His East Market hardware store became Stockenberg's for many years and is now owned by Richard and Carleen Stockenberg Bayright. It houses the Williams Lumber Hardware Store. EBHSRH Archives.

Life in a Mid-19th Century Village

The tinsmith, John Curtis, who also co-owned a hardware store on East Market Street kept a diary from the 1830s through the 1850s. In its pages is a rare glimpse of life in small town, rural New York, with many of its rough edges. In the winter of 1838, when Curtis's wife was ill, he had to care for her and their four children, with the help of a "hired girl," about whom he had constant complaints. The family lived in a nice two-story house, since demolished, which stood east of what is now the Key Bank on West Market Street. Besides running the store, installing tin roofs and peddling tinware around town with his horse and cart, Curtis tried his hand one evening at making oyster stew. It fed his family for a week. The roads in Red Hook were unpaved, and that year, full of mud.

"Rain and fog," he wrote despondently in an entry on January 14, 1848, "times dull, very dull, uncommonly dull, exceedingly dull, excessively dull! Went to Barrytown and overhauled the old inn. Sold six stoves this week."

Life could be, apparently, very boring, and Curtis threw himself into attending church revivals at the Methodist Church, and in organizing a 12-week lecture series at the Lutheran Church Hall in the winter of 1854. The famous publisher Horace Greeley spoke on "Reform and Reformers." "The house was not large enough!" a delighted John Curtis exclaimed in his diary next day.

St. Paul's Hall: This Lutheran parish hall, a fine example of the decorated Gothic style of architecture, replaced an earlier building called the Lecture Hall in 1884, the same year the new church went up. The community used both halls, as John Curtis did in the 1850s, for lectures and programs. Fred Briggs Collection.

Numerous entries note the illness or death of relatives and neighbors in the 1850s. Two entries in November 1855, were sad and succinct, "Willie died today…. Today we lost Mollie." Within one week, his own two young children had succumbed to scarlet fever.[33]

Bird's Eye View c. 1890: The large brick commercial blocks, including the Massoneau building (1855, near corner), the Conklin and Allendorf building (1879, far corner) and the large tobacco factory (c. 1830, near right) established the village as Red Hook's center by the 1880s. Note the tall pole used to fly flags forecasting weather. Losee Collection.

Chapter 10
The Civil War

We know that over 500 men enlisted from Red Hook between 1861 and 1865 to fight in the "Slave Holders Rebellion," according to unusually meticulous records kept by General J. Watts DePeyster of Tivoli. They were distributed among at least 47 regiments and four war vessels. A memorial erected by DePeyster in 1866 in Tivoli, lists sixteen men killed in action and thirteen more who died of disease or their wounds shortly after the war.

Virgil Group: The son of Nicholas Group, who farmed at the corner of Benner Road and West Market Street. Virgil was one of many local boys who went off to quash the "slaveholder's rebellion." Maynard Ham Collection.

The young men who left town to fight seemed full of patriotism and home pride. Corporal Edward Holt of the 7th New York Infantry, stationed in Camp Hill, Washington, wrote to thank Red Hook citizens for their generous care packages, including a large fruit cake, nine pairs of gloves, cigars and chewing tobacco from the local factory, a package of pears and a barrel of apples, onions and sweet potatoes. wrote Holt:

The pears were eaten with hearty good will. The apples… from John W. Allendorf, were very fine indeed—and the onions and potatoes were the nicest we have seen since our arrival here…. Frequent remarks were made by those of our company from New Jersey… as to the liberality of the inhabitants of Red Hook village."[34]

Holt, later promoted to orderly sergeant, was wounded at Gettysburg.

More descriptive of the miseries of war was a letter from C.S. Wilber, stranded in quarantine on the Steamer Arago for four months in Florida. Many died from disease and the rough trip down the stormy east coast. Wilber wrote:

During our stay on ship we lived on crackers so hard that we had to lay them down on the deck and break them with our heel, and stick the worms with a bayonet as they were attempting to crawl off. We had not a bit of water except that condensed from the boiler, and even that was sickening to drink."[35]

There were always those who sought to stay put. Able-bodied men from Red Hook have gone to Poughkeepsie to get certificates of exemption, wrote one critic. "Every complaint in the catalogue of diseases was brought forward, Consumption, Rheumatism and cross eyes; and some are said to have a complaint called the "Green Piles," (a twenty dollar green-back) which exempts them from draft. What an army of cripples and invalids the drafted army will be!"[36]

Chapter 11
The Legacy of the Great Estates

*t*he stately houses rising on the shore of town between 1790 and 1940, stood linked by history and kin like a jeweled necklace along the river. Architecturally and geographically, they towered over the adjacent properties and modest homes in the villages. Most of the big houses were surrounded by farms and landscaped gardens of three-or four-hundred acres or more. Beside their obvious beauty, however, they contributed to town life in some practical ways. They became an increasing source of employment for local workers in the 19th century, when many of the old places underwent extensive renovations and expansions of their farming operations. In addition, many of the estate owners, following the tradition of their class in the 19th and early 20th centuries, sought to "improve" the lives of their workers, and the surrounding community, primarily though religion and education. Often they became benefactors to the community, building churches and schools for their employees and their families in the neighborhood as well as for their own. These structures were often designed by the same prominent architects they employed to create their own estates, with the same attention to style and detail. This trend, especially prominent in the mid- to late-19th century, resulted in an unusually high number of fine "cottages," and public buildings still to be seen in Red Hook. Many remain as examples of the 19th century Romantic Landscape Movement, which had its roots in Red Hook.

An Architectural Legacy: In Annandale, the octagonal Blithewood Gatehouse, (above) designed by Alexander Jackson Davis for Robert Donaldson, is an administrative building at Bard College today. A.J. Davis designed the cottage (above right) in the mid-1800s. It is now owned by Bard College. The DePeyster Fireman's Hall (right) was built by J.W. DePeyster of Rose Hill in 1898 and given to the Village of Tivoli. Tivoli raised $1.4 million to restore it in 1995, for village offices, a museum and community center. These are just a few examples of the legacy of public and private buildings left by the estate owners over the years. Photos by Douglas Baz.

The Donaldsons and the Aspinwalls at Barrytown, the Bards at Annandale and Tivoli, the Livingstons at Tivoli and the Astors in Red Hook, all built or primarily financed the construction of schools and churches that remain prominent in the town today. Many public buildings went up in the 19th century. General John DePeyster, proprietor of *Rose Hill*, built the Methodist Church as well as the expansive firemen's hall in the Village of Tivoli. The J. Watts DePeyster Fireman's Hall on Main Street was restored by the community in the 1990s and serves today as the official village hall.

The Episcopalians seem to have been the most active in establishing schools in Red Hook. The first Episcopal congregation in the town, the second Episcopal congregation in Dutchess County after St. James in Hyde Park, was organized in 1816 in Tivoli, with the support of Edward P. and John S. Livingston. St. Paul's Episcopal church was established in a simple, white clapboard building at the intersection of the Road to Germantown (Route 9G) and the Road to Tivoli (Broadway in Tivoli, once an extension of West Kerley's Corner's Road). It was called the White Church, to distinguish it from the Dutch Reformed "Red Church," just up the road. It's successor the beautiful Norman Gothic stone Church of St. Paul's that stands today on Woods Road was built in 1868.

The "new" Methodist Episcopal Church and Parsonage: In 1893, this Victorian-style church replaced an original A.J. Davis design commissioned by Mrs. Edward Livingston of Montgomery Place. The church was built at the corner of West Market and Church streets, on farmland given by Phillip Gilbert Fraleigh. Note the Victorian detail, enhanced by the painting. EBHSRH Archives.

St. Paul's Episcopal Church: In 1818 the first "White Church," was located at the northwest corner of West Kerleys Corners Road and Route 9G. This church was built in 1868 on Woods Road on land given by Eugene Livingston and J. Watts DePeyster. Losee Collection.

Bard College

One of the most prominent institutions in town—Bard College—started out as an Episcopal seminary, the work of two great promoters of education and the Episcopal Church, John Bard and his wife, Margaret. The Bards bought *Blithewood* from Robert Donaldson in 1853, and renamed the house Annandale, effectively changing the name of the 18th century hamlet, Cedar Hill, as well. The Bards immediately built a small school, now called *Bard Hall*, where Margaret Bard taught local children. First operated as a church school, it later became the first public school house in Annandale. Around the same time, the Bards also erected Trinity School, a church school in Tivoli, and employed a teacher to head both programs. By 1857, a small group of older students began studying for the Episcopal priesthood at the Annandale school. Encouraged by the Episcopal bishop of New York, the Bards decided to fund the building of St. Stephen's

Theological Seminary in 1860. The college became affiliated with Columbia University in 1928 for several years, and in 1934, changed its name to Bard College. At that time it ceased to prepare students exclusively for the priesthood. It became co-educational in 1948, and developed a reputation as a progressive college of Liberal Arts. In the 1980s it developed master's programs in the arts, education and the environment. It continues to be associated with the Episcopal Church.

St. Margaret's Well: St. Stephen's graduating class c. 1884, poses before the well named in honor of Margaret Bard. Bard Hall (on the right) was first constructed by Margaret and John Bard in 1854 as a school for local children. Margaret taught at Bard Hall for many years. When the couple founded St. Stephen's six years later, Margaret Bard became one of the first women in the country to serve on a college board of trustees. Bard College Archives.

A Thank Offering and a Memorial

About the time the Bards established their little country school, their only son, Willie, was born. The grateful parents built the beautiful Gothic Chapel of the Holy Innocents in 1857 next to Bard Hall as a thank offering for their son. The church had just been completed and ready for use when it caught fire in December of 1858 and burned to the ground. Work on the new church of stone began immediately and was completed in 1860, the same year that plans for the new college were completed. Margaret Bard, who was an advocate for education in her own right, was named with her husband in the college's charter and designated one of the Charter trustees, unusual honors at the time for a woman.

St. Stephen's classroom: Robed students attend class on the third floor of Aspinwall Hall in 1880, at the Episcopal seminary founded by patron John Bard in 1860. St. Stephen's Theological Seminary became Bard College in the 1930s. Students wore their academic robes well into the 20th century. Bard College Archives.

Church of the Holy Innocents. Built a year before Bard founded St. Stephen's this Episcopal Chapel was dedicated to the Bard's only son, Willie. It became the chapel to the college, and remains so today. Bard is still affiliated with the Episcopal Church colleges. Photo by Tom Daley.

Trinity Church in Tivoli: The church, which still stands on North Road as a private home, served the local Episcopalians and was the predecessor of Trinity School For Boys. Tivoli Archives.

In 1868, the lovely chapel, which had been dedicated to their son's birth, became a memorial to him, when, at the age of 12 years, he died suddenly of "malignant fever."[37] Grief stricken, the Bards left for England, where they lived for the rest of their lives, returning to the college they founded only as occasional visitors. A small white marble stone, cut above the sacristy door on the outside of the church, dedicates the chapel to the little boy.

Bard College has grown from a student body of six students gathered at Bard Hall on the day it opened in September of 1860, to approximately 1,250 undergraduate and over 200 graduate students on a campus that spans over 540 acres. Under the leadership of today's college president, Leon Botstein, who was the youngest president of an American college, and has developed Bard College into one of America's outstanding liberal arts colleges.

Schools and Homes

When John Bard built Trinity Episcopal Church and school several miles north in Tivoli, he employed the Reverend James Starr Clark to run them both. This led to the establishment of Trinity Episcopal School for Boys, one of the largest and longest-running church schools in the area. It eventually expanded into a boarding school that housed 50 students, drawn from many states and abroad. It became the DePeyster Industrial Home for Girls in the 20th century, supported by and named for its benefactor, John Watts DePeyster of *Rose Hill.* The school was demolished in 1938. The old church building is now a private residence.

Two other homes for orphaned or poor children were established by local families. In 1905, DePeyster transferred ownership of his home, *Rose Hill,* to the Leake and Watts Children's Home, an orphanage with branches in New York City and Yonkers. It operated for 40 years in Tivoli before being sold. In the 1940s, it was bought by Dorothy Day of the Catholic Worker movement. She operated the house as a summer retreat for Catholic Workers until her death in 1980. Dorothy Day is currently under consideration by the Vatican for sainthood.

DePeyster Industrial Home for Girls: The building housed the Trinity School for Boys for 25 years, before J.W. DePeyster opened his home for girls in 1892. The home was connected with the Methodists' Home Missionary Society. In 1900 there were 60 students there. It was demolished in 1938. Tivoli Archives.

The Astors of *Rokeby* established St. Margaret's Orphan Asylum in 1853. Built south of the Village of Red Hook, it was the first private institution of its kind in the county, founded to look after disadvantaged children. St. Margaret's was built during a farm recession, a period when local farmers often had difficulty supporting their large families, especially girls, who were not considered as much of an asset as a boy when it came to farm work. In the fashion of the time, these neglected local girls were trained in housekeeping, cooking and child rearing, and often were employed as paid domestic servants in the surrounding estates or the homes of prosperous local families. The Astors, followed by their descendants, the Chanlers and the Aldriches, supported the home and its management by Christ Episcopal Church until the late 1930s, when St. Margaret's Home was shut down and sold.

St. Margaret's: Girls housed at "Mrs. Astor's Orphan Asylum," were not always orphans, but the daughters of families who could not afford to keep them. It was built in 1854 by Margaret Armstrong, who had grown up at Rokeby and married William B. Astor. St. Margaret's in 1934. Located on Route 9, it is now unused. EBHSRH Archives.

St. John the Evangelist

The Aspinwalls came to live at *Massena* in 1860 and, like their neighbors, the Bards, were strong Episcopalians. John Aspinwall helped found St. Stephen's in 1860. He was also involved in St. Peter's Brotherhood, a missionary arm of the college. Through the Brotherhood, young seminarians from St. Stephens would instruct local youngsters in the Bible and other religious subjects. They built St. Peter's Chapel at the crossroads of Budd's Corners and Whaleback Road in Red

St. John the Evangelist, Barrytown: The Episcopal church, built in 1874. St. John's continues a long-standing historical and spriritual connection to Bard College. Photo by Len Vogler.

Hook, where they held classes and services. It was later moved to form part of St. John the Evangelist in Barrytown.

After Aspinwall's death in 1874, his wife, Jane, built the Free Episcopal Church of St. John the Evangelist as a memorial to him. The beautiful Carpenter Gothic-style wooden church, designed by William A. Potter, served the employees of the surrounding estates, who had little transport outside of Barrytown. One local, elderly parishioner recalled her mother's story of the horse-drawn side-seater sent around each Sunday by the Aspinwalls to collect people to go to church.[38]

In the 1880s, St. John's established another mission, All Saints Chapel, in Upper Red Hook. For many years it was connected with the adjacent property, St. Clare's House. Originally called *Lyle House,* it was one of the earliest and grandest of the houses in Upper Red Hook, a three-story gambrel-roofed 18th century Dutch house built at the corner of the road to Spring Lake. In the 19th century, it was the home of celebrated painter Edward L. Mooney and his daughter, Ella. The house was passed down to her companion, Ina Russell. The two women were patrons of All Saints and taught Sunday School there. Following their deaths the property became St. Clare's House, a home for retired Episcopal deaconesses, endowed by the Mooney estate. It operated for about 15 years. Both St. Clare's and the chapel were closed and sold by Christ Church in the 1950s.

All Saint's Chapel: In 1886, St. John's and the Aspinwall family established a chapel in Upper Red Hook as a mission to the Barrytown Church. Patrons of All Saints, the Misses Ella Mooney and Ina Russell, taught Sunday School there for many years. The Baptismal Record from 1912 contains the names of families still found in Red Hook. Red Hook Christ Episcopal Church Archives.

In Barrytown: Two Chapels and a School

The Robert Donaldson family, owners of *Edgewater* in the late 1850s, was responsible for the construction of the town's only Presbyterian church—Sylvania Chapel—and a Roman Catholic church—Sacred Heart, both in Barrytown. This was, however, after an unusual family crisis.

Sylvania Chapel: A.J. Davis designed this small Presbyterian chapel for Robert Donaldson in 1856. Donaldson is buried in the yard. It became a Lutheran Chapel, then was sold to Alan Porter, a well-remembered personality locally and the original creator of the New York Museum of Modern Art Film Festival. Greta Garbo was his occasional guest. Photo by Tom Daley.

Church of the Sacred Heart: Built in 1875 by the Catholic children of the Protestant Robert Donaldson on Station Hill Road in Barrytown. By that time, the church was very much needed for the growing number of Irish Catholics who had come to work on the railroad and estates. Losee Collection.

In 1855 Donaldson hired architect A.J. Davis to design the small Sylvania Chapel, which still stands off Dock Road, for use by the children of the village and his own family. Donaldson was a Presbyterian who had married a Catholic. His children, raised as Protestants, attended services and Sunday school faithfully at Sylvania Chapel, until the day of their planned confirmation, when they announced publicly that they were Roman Catholic, according to one family story. Unbeknownst to Donaldson, their mother had privately taught them her family faith. It apparently came as a complete surprise to Donaldson. He was so shaken by the development that he disinherited all three of his children in his will. After he died in 1872, a lawsuit restored the family fortune to them.[39]

St. Sylvia's Roman Catholic Church: The first Catholic services were held at a white wooden church down at the Tivoli landing around 1852. The present church was built in 1903 in memory of Mrs. Johnston Livingston by her daughters, Mrs. Geraldyn Redmond and Countess deLaugier-Villars. EBHSRH Archives.

In those days, all area Roman Catholics had to cross the river to attend services in Kingston, unless they wanted to travel to St. Sylvia's Roman Catholic Church, which had been built in Tivoli following an influx of Irish Catholic railroad workers in 1852 (the present Church of St. Sylvia's was donated to the village by the Redmonds of *Callendar House* in the early 20th century). Otherwise, they could make the trip to Rhinebeck to worship at St. Joseph's in Rhinecliff.

One Sunday in 1875, as a group of Catholics was crossing the river to go to Mass, there was a tragic boating accident. Moved by the deaths, the Catholic children of Robert Donaldson donated a parcel of land and built the little Catholic Church of the Sacred Heart. They also donated the steeply sloping hill on which was built the Catholic cemetery. The church closed its doors in the 1970s, as had Sylvania Chapel many years before. Both are now private dwellings.

Barrytown School House: Designed by A.J. Davis and built in 1857 by Robert Donaldson, the building served as District #8's public schoolhouse for 82 years, until it was closed in 1939 to join the Red Hook Central District. It is now a private dwelling. EBHSRH Archives.

Following the example of the Bards, and responding to the growing number of children in Barrytown, Robert Donaldson commissioned A.J. Davis to build a public schoolhouse in Barrytown, just east of what is now Station Hill Road, in 1855. It is now a private home.

Just down the road in Annandale, the Bards built Bard Hall a few years later to serve as a one-room public school. Before St. Stephens College was conceived, local children walked to class to be taught by Margaret Bard each day.

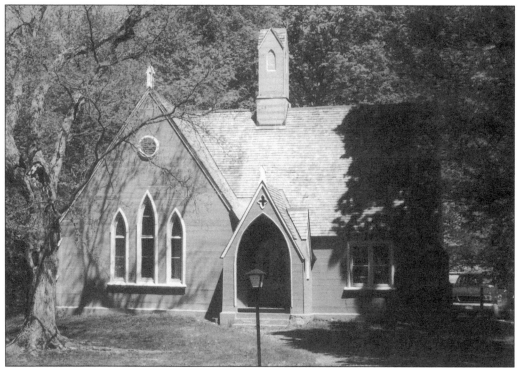

Bard Hall: Built in 1857 by John and Margaret Bard, as a school for local children, this small gothic-style wooden structure is the oldest building on Bard Campus. Margaret Bard was its first teacher. It still serves students as a recital and lecture hall for Bard College. Photo by Tom Daley.

Chapter 12
Red Hook Peaks in Farming and Industry

*b*eginning in the early 1800s, and peaking in the years before and after the Civil War, Red Hook developed into a very lively manufacturing town. Throughout the late 19th century, small factories and shops produced chewing tobacco and cigars, cocoa and cooking chocolate, leather, furniture, harness, wagons and tinplate. The seasonal river industries included harvesting and storing ice in winter and fishing for sturgeon, shad and herring in spring and summer, all for transport to the city. Besides shoeing their horses, blacksmiths produced iron tools and implements for local farmers.

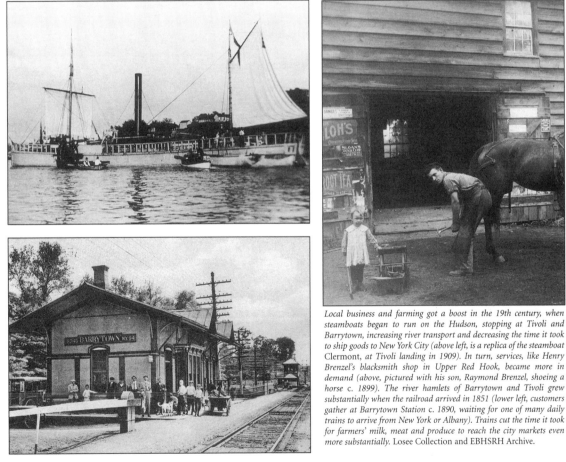

Local business and farming got a boost in the 19th century, when steamboats began to run on the Hudson, stopping at Tivoli and Barrytown, increasing river transport and decreasing the time it took to ship goods to New York City (above left, is a replica of the steamboat Clermont, at Tivoli landing in 1909). In turn, services, like Henry Brenzel's blacksmith shop in Upper Red Hook, became more in demand (above, pictured with his son, Raymond Brenzel, shoeing a horse c. 1899). The river hamlets of Barrytown and Tivoli grew substantially when the railroad arrived in 1851 (lower left, customers gather at Barrytown Station c. 1890, waiting for one of many daily trains to arrive from New York or Albany). Trains cut the time it took for farmers' milk, meat and produce to reach the city markets even more substantially. Losee Collection and EBHSRH Archive.

Beginning in the 1850s, the Hudson River Railroad, built along Red Hook's shoreline, created new jobs in construction, freighting, and related industries. Businesses sprang up in all the hamlets and around the landings. The old ferry landings that had served the town since the early 1700s were transformed into passenger and freight centers for steamboat and rail traffic, and the populations of the river hamlets peaked.

Just 18 months after the Hudson River Railroad opened for business in Red Hook in October of 1851, there were three passenger trains daily from New York to Red Hook, reaching Barrytown in three and one-half hours. A round-trip ticket cost $1.40.[40] By 1868, the schedule had increased service to six northbound and six southbound trains daily.

New people settled in the area, especially the Irish, altering the makeup of the Dutch, German and English names that had dominated the town census rolls for 100 years.

Around the mid-19th century, Red Hook began to develop quite differently from neighboring Rhinebeck. Besides the tobacco factory, the town reported twice as many industrial and commercial operations as Rhinebeck in 1850 and in 1870. Red Hook had 24 manufacturing businesses, ranging from mills, blacksmiths and small wagon and carriage making shops that employed between two and four workers, to the relatively large tobacco and tin manufacturers, employing between 40 and 50 people. Red Hook firms employed 179 men and 21 women in 1850. Wages from the Red Hook industrial shops averaged $30 a month for a skilled carriage maker to $14 a month for a mill worker, cooper and tinmaker.

There were two tin manufacturers operating in the village—Orison Graves and J.B. Curtis. Curtis was in operation for 30 years. In 1898, William H. Baker produced chocolate and cocoa at their factory in Annandale, employing 25 men and 19 women and girls. By 1900, they had moved to Red Hook Village.[41]

The Red Hook Tobacco Company

The tobacco industry in Red Hook was established by the Massonneau family, French immigrants who in 1812 built a store at the four corners on a piece of property bought from John Armstrong. Claudius Massonneau built the tobacco factory just south of the store around 1830, though an early account of the family business indicates chewing tobacco and cigars were manufactured by the Massonneaus even earlier. At the factory, Robert Livingston Massonneau started the practice of reading aloud to workers who would sit and tediously roll tobacco into cigars. Many were women, with the heavier jobs of cutting, packing and drying going to men. In the early years, tobacco was brought up to Barrytown by sloop in summer and by horse and sleigh along the roads in winter.

Red Hook Tobacco Factory: The clapboard building, topped with a bell tower that rang the noontime hour, as well as the start and end of the business day, was a major presence in the commercial life of the lower village in the 19th and early 20th century. The business employed scores of workers. Photo, c. 1890. Losee Collection.

Writing about those early years, William Massonneau noted:

When a couple of hogsheads of tobacco came to the Barrytown dock, it was sent for with a large wagon and four horses... Sometimes a bugler on horseback was sent ahead to announce its coming as it was considered a noteworthy event... The tobacco was taken to the old store building, where it was cut up finely by hand and packed in barrels, or small packages, when it was taken out on the road for sale. Barter was pretty generally used in those days, and the wagons brought back (to the Barrytown dock) butter, honey, hides and even lumber, which in turn was sold.[42]

Red Hook Tobacco: The red hook and bucket was the brand symbol of the Red Hook Tobacco Co., and later, Hoffman & Company Tobacco. Maynard Ham Collection.

This humidor contained cigars manufactured at the factory in Red Hook, from 1812 to the 1930s. Losee Collection.

In 1850, the factory, operated by J & P Hendricks, employed 30 men and eight women to work 10-hour days, with women earning an average of $12 a month, and men, $20. Some women were employed to roll cigars at home for piecework. Throughout the century, a bell atop the factory, which has since been lost, tolled the starting and closing times and the noon hour for workers and residents of the village. The factory produced one million cigars in 1850, and 200,000 pounds of chewing tobacco under the brand names, "Red Hook," "Deer Head," "Yellow Spot," and "Eagle."[43]

The business continued to be a major employer in the village and produced chewing and smoking tobacco and snuff until the 1930s. The new Pennsylvania firm that bought the company continued production under the brand name "Red Hook Tobacco" for years.

Farming Flourished

Blessed by very good soils, especially inland (the soil was rich loam, mixed with clay by the river), and with the Northeast cold moderated by the Hudson River, Red Hook farming flourished, reaching its peak in the last quarter of the century. Farmers could ship meat, cheese, poultry, fruit and vegetables to New York City in four hours by train. Each evening local farmers met the milk train at Barrytown or Tivoli, sending off their milk and butter in time to reach the city market when it opened

A Relaxing Moment: Resting at the Philip Fraleigh Farm on Fraleigh Lane, c. 1895. The house dates to the late 1700s. The mid to late 19th century was a peak period of productivity at local farms, which dominated the economy until around World War II. Fraleigh Collection.

next day at 5 a.m. Hay, grain and bedding straw were also shipped to support the vast population of horses in the pre-auto, pre-subway city.

Burton Coon, writing about his boyhood on a farm near Red Hook in the 1870s, recalled his father's description of meeting the boat at Barrytown in the early part of the century: "I have heard almost unbelievable stories of the immense amount of pork coming down to the river from back in the country, even as far away as Connecticut;… teams would be in line from Barrytown dock as far back as the four corners (River Road), waiting for a chance to unload."[44] Apples were shipped in this way too, before the establishment of the big commercial orchards in the late 1800s. Barrels of apples were taken to the Barrytown dock, put on barges like *The Sarah Smith* in charge of the captain, and sold in New York with no charge for the captain's services.

Milk Delivery: John Fraleigh of Rose Hill farm, pictured with his son, made his milk run each day in the late 1800s. He is stopped here in front of the Methodist Church on Church Street, c. 1890. The Fraleighs have farmed in Red Hook for over 200 years. Fraleigh Collection.

Steamboat Ad: The barge Sarah Smith, *the steamboat,* Saugerties *and the steamer,* Ulster, *made weekly stops at Barrytown and Tivoli to drop off and pick up produce and passengers. Red Hook Journal, 1898. Maynard Ham Collection.*

Monmouth Pippen, Blackgilliflower and Winter Banana

Apple Harvest: Pickers at the Losee Farm in Upper Red Hook, c. 1920. Migrant workers, who followed the harvests from Florida to Maine, were used at local farms beginning in the 1920s. Before that, pickers were hired from the local population. Losee Collection.

In 1875, Red Hook reported 30,517 apple trees, producing 22,640 bushels of apples and 1200 gallons of apple cider. Its vineyards and orchards produced 39,375 pounds of grapes, as well as peaches and pears.[45] There were 90 varieties of apples and 20 varieties of pears displayed by Red Hook farmers at the Dutchess County Fair in 1902.[46] As late as 1954, right before a general decline in agriculture in the region, Red Hook apple farmers produced 328,128 bushels of the popular varietes, MacIntosh, Cortlandt, Rome, Ida Red, Northern Spy, and Red and Golden Delicious —an indication of the importance of apples to the town's economy. By point of comparison, Rhinebeck produced just 10,662 bushels that year.[47]

Burton Coon remembered the 1870s as the beginning of the big commercial fruit operations. No spraying was done in those early years, the market was not overcrowded and the fruit was "quite fair," with less insects and blight. Hundreds of varieties of apples were grown in the Hudson Valley, with wonderful names that have faded in memory: Newtown and Monmouth Pippin, Maiden Blush, Twenty Ounce, Pumpkin Sweet, Black Gilliflower, Seek No Further and Winter Banana. One variety common to Red Hook in 1908 was called the Striped Ox.[48] In the 1870s, an entire orchard of Newtown Pippins on the Feller farm in Red Hook was sold to a dealer for $1,000, a remarkable price at the time. "They were good apples too," wrote Coon of the once popular Monmouth, or "Mammoth" Pippin, "coloring to a rich golden yellow with a red cheek, in the spring."[49]

Taking Care of the Harvest: Horsedrawn rigs like this one were introduced around 1915 to spray pesticides on apples to protect against disease and blight. The handheld wand had a nozzle at the end (left). Around 1930, at the Losee farm the whole family was called upon to pick and pack apples, before winter set in (right). They were taken each afternoon to catch the "night train" in Barrytown or Tivoli, in order to reach New York markets by early morning. Losee Collection.

The Hucklebush

The Central New England Railroad, locally called the Hucklebush, opened for business in 1870. It ran east from Rhinecliff through Red Hook and Cokertown to Connecticut, carrying milk and produce for farmers and materials for manufacturers. Nicknamed Chamberlain's Folly, for the Red Hook landowner and New York City merchant William Chamberlain of Maizefield who fought to get it built, the Hucklebush was probably never a paying proposition. But it was important to the town's economy—especially for transportation of farm products and raw materials for local industrial shops. The Hucklebush picked up passengers and milk from the dairy farms at country

The Red Hook Depot c. 1910: The Central New England Railroad, called locally the Hucklebush, ran from Rhinecliff, east to Connecticut. The Red Hook station took on passengers, milk, chocolate products and farm produce to ship to New York City and out of state markets. Losee Collection.

sidings east and west of the village (Spring Lake and Fraleigh's farm are two examples) on its way to New England or to connect with the Hudson River Railroad at Rhinecliff. For more than 60 years, the milk train stopped daily at the Red Hook depot at the end of Elizabeth Street in the Village. Agway occupies what was the railroad's freight house. There it would deliver milk to the Baker's Chocolate Factory, one of the largest operations in Red Hook. The Hucklebush ran a passenger service until the 1930s.

The Chocolate Factory

Though many hotels, stores and even mill sites changed hands or went in and out of operation relatively quickly in the 19th century, there were a few noteworthy exceptions, the tobacco factory, in operation at least 90 years, being one of them, and the W.H. Baker's Chocolate Factory, being another. The business was established in Annandale on the upper Saw Kill falls around 1880. In 1898 it employed 25 men, 14 women and five girls under the age of 21.[50] The factory switched from water power to steam power around 1900, and moved to the village. The company built its new factory right next to the railroad, taking advantage of the faster transport system. It stayed in operation until the 1920s, producing baking chocolate and cocoa, and utilizing locally produced dairy products. In 1913, it was employed 79 adults and three children under 16 years old. The large stone and brick building still stands at the base of Thompson Street in the Village, near what was once the railroad depot for the Hucklebush line. The chocolate factory has been restored and contains several businesses.

W.H. Baker Chocolate Factory: For over 40 years the chocolate factory employed local men and women to produce cooking chocolate, using the milk from local farms. (Beginning lower right and proceeding counter-clockwise) The business was first established in 1890 on the Saw Kill in Annandale. Workers at the Annandale plant pose for their portrait c. 1895. The business then moved to Red Hook Village, near the CNERR station at the end of Thompson Street. Today the building is owned by Dr. George Verrilli and was recently renovated to accommodate a number of businesses and arts and crafts shops. W.H. Baker Chocolate Factory in Annandale photos from Ruth and Frank Oja; W.H. Baker Chocolate Factory, Losee Collection; and The Chocolate Factory photo by Douglas Baz.

The Borden Milk Company operated a creamery, bottling plant and bulk shipping operation there until the 1960s, taking advantage of the rail and later truck transport, and using the milk supply from local dairy farms.

Bonaparte's Sheep

Red Hook produced a lot of high quality fleece throughout the 19th century. Wool production, which was much higher in Red Hook than surrounding towns, was not so much affected by better soils as it was by history. In 1849, nearly 1,500 sheep produced 8,850 pounds of "clipp" in Red Hook, compared to 4,900 pounds from about 1,000 sheep in Rhinebeck.[51] The difference in the number of sheep does not account for Red Hook's heavier clipp, which is a word for the weight of the fleece. However, this was the same town that saw the introduction of the Spanish Merinos in the late 1700s, when Chancellor Livingston and his brother John R. Livingston of Massena established the breed in Red Hook. In 1811 their brother-in-law, General Armstrong, brought from France a gift of the fine, thick-wooled sheep from Napoleon Bonaparte, inspiring him to name his new farm, "LaBergerie," the sheep-fold. The characteristics of the Merino sheep, and its heavy fleece, could account for the higher wool production seen consistently in Red Hook flocks in the 19th century.

In 1918, the state Agricultural Department in Albany valued farmland in Red Hook at between $40 and $200 an acre, more than twice the value of Rhinebeck's farmland, which was valued at $30 to $80 an acre.[52]

Bird's Eye View from the Red Hook Chocolate Factory: Taken from the tower of the factory near the village depot, looking northwest, c. 1890. This overview shows the relative sparseness of most of the rural village. Practically every house had a large vegetable garden and a berry patch or grape vines. Household chickens and small penned animals were also common in backyards, and streets were unpaved. Note the violet greenhouses. EBHSRH Archives.

Chapter 13
Barrytown

*I*n the mid-19th century, the Lower Red Hook Landing, which had been a commercial point along the river since the mid-1700s, finally received a name when U.S. Postmaster General William Barry, agreed to establish a post office in the hamlet in 1830, so long as it bore the name of this Kentucky politician.

Nineteenth Century Barrytown: This engraving taken from a Federal Navigation Handbook in 1880, shows the landing at Barrytown with Edgewater on the right. It became a lively place of trade, and freight transport in the early 19th century. Rokeby Collection.

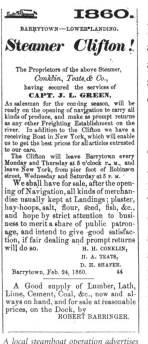

1860.

BARRYTOWN—LOWER LANDING.

Steamer *Clifton!*

The Proprietors of the above Steamer,
Conklin, Teats & Co.,
having secured the services of
CAPT. J. L. GREEN,

As salesman for the coming season, will be ready on the opening of navigation to carry all kinds of produce, and make as prompt returns as any other Freighting Establishment on the river. In addition to the Clifton we have a receiving Boat in New York, which will enable us to get the best prices for all articles entrusted to our care.

The Clifton will leave Barrytown every Monday and Thursday at 5 o'clock P. M., and leave New York, from pier foot of Robinson street, Wednesday and Saturday at 5 P. M.

We shall have for sale, after the opening of Navigation, all kinds of merchandise usually kept at Landings; plaster, hay-hoops, salt, flour, seed, fish, &c., and hope by strict attention to business to merit a share of public patronage, and intend to give good satisfaction, if fair dealing and prompt returns will do so.　　　H. H. CONKLIN,
　　　　　　　H. A. TEATS,
　　　　　　　D. H. SHAFER.
Barrytown, Feb. 24, 1860.　　44

A Good supply of Lumber, Lath, Lime, Cement, Coal, &c., now and always on hand, and for sale at reasonable prices, on the Dock, by
　　ROBERT BARRINGER.

A local steamboat operation advertises in 1860 in the Red Hook Journal. *Maynard Ham Collection.*

Barrytown was a passenger and freight stop for the new Hudson River Railroad, and became a lively place of business. In addition to the post office, there were two docks, several hotels, a general store, blacksmith shop, cooperage, icehouses, a railroad station, railway express agency, telegraph office, railroad traffic control tower, and a steamboat wharf.

The steamboats at Barrytown and Tivoli continued to operate, despite competition from the railroad, until the 1920s. Advertisements for the steam ships and their schedules appeared regularly in the local newspapers, along with railroad schedules. The boats still delivered mail to Barrytown in mid-century, as well as hauled passengers and freight. They had the added advantage, on a run to New York City, of providing transport for a passenger's horse and carriage, as well—if he wanted to pay the price. By 1870, the population at the Barrytown lower landing peaked at 350 residents, "a place of considerable trade," as was noted in the annual "New York State Gazetteer."

When the ice froze in winter, ice harvesting began, providing major seasonal employment. Two ice houses at Barrytown—the Mutual Ice Company, a large, insulated building, and the Livingston Ice House, a smaller wooden structure— had a combined storage capacity of 88,000 pounds of ice, most of it bound for New York City kitchens.[53] Block ice was shipped during the warm seasons in insulated barges. In winter, it was sawn into 300-pound blocks with the help of horse-drawn cutting plows, then floated in a channel cut through the river ice to a steam powered conveyor, which lifted them into the icehouse. The daily wage of about $1.75 for this dangerous labor was considered good money. At the end of the day, farmers could be seen leaving the dock in "long lines of sleighs and in much hilarity on the way home."[54]

Harvesting the ice at Barrytown: Men worked into the night if the moon was full in order to cut and load ice into storage when temperatures were low enough for a deep freeze on the river. This engraving (left) was featured in Frank Leslie's Illustrated Newspaper, 1871, *The ice was packed and stored in large ice houses (right) like this one in 1901, owned by the Consolidated Ice Company. From there, steamboat barges transported the ice throughout the year for sale to New York City. Properly packed ice kept for months, even in summer. Keith Denegar Collection and Rokeby Collection.*

Israel Snyder's Cooperage: This shop, which made and repaired wooden barrels, tubs and casks, was located next to the public school (in background) on the road to Barrytown dock. It was convenient for wagon teams carrying produce to and from the steamboat dock or the railroad. 1881. EBHSRH Archives.

Shoeing a Team c. 1880: The Navins Brothers Blacksmith Shop stood at Barrytown Corners in the 1880s. Teams of horses hauled freight to and from the river landing and later the train station. The location at the corner of River Road and Barrytown Road, was good for business. Losee Collection.

Secondary industries sprang up at the Barrytown Corners, where a blacksmith shop operated from the 1850s to the 1880s. Israel Snyder's cooperage shop also lasted more than 30 years, selling farmers passing through the barrels they needed for freighting.

It appeared however that prosperity—even relative prosperity—often failed to deliver the mail on time. In the 1860s, as today, it was part of daily life to await the delivery of the daily mail. At rural stops like Barrytown it was the habit to throw the mailbag off the mail train as it went by the station on its daily run between Albany and New York. Sometimes the postal clerk would miss by "a country mile," dropping it at the wrong station and making some residents pine for the slower, more reliable steamboat service. A Red Hook resident registered her complaint with wilting criticism in "The Red Hook Journal:"

> *Does not the new mail Agent on the Hudson River Road know that there is a mail station at Barrytown.... It is a splendid arrangement indeed, if all this region of country must be deprived of its regular mail until it gets twenty-four hours old, while the agent takes it along up the road and throws it off where he pleases. If you want to make a community 'ripping mad,' just withhold their mail facilities for a few days...(if) this is to be the permanent arrangement, then we go in at once for chartering a scow, or clam boat to bring up the mail from New York, that we may get it at least in twelve hours.*[55]

In 1881, an icehouse fire devastated the commercial riverfront. Residents rebuilt, but fire struck again in 1908, destroying most of the industrial buildings and some residences. Neither the commerce, nor the industry ever recovered.

Red Hook Farm Life: The Vosburghs of Upper Red Hook are posed here c. 1890, in front of their farmhouse. It appears, that the family and their neighbor, photographer, farmer, and inveterate recorder of Red Hook rural life, Will Teator, decided to have fun posing one summer's day with all the implements of their labor and leisure. Will Teater Collection.

Chapter 14
Tivoli Merger:
"Good Order, Good Walks"

In Tivoli, where Robert Fulton's steamboat had already brought about a lively freight trade in farm produce and ice beginning in the 1830s, the population swelled significantly with the influx of railroad workers in the 1840s and 1850s. By 1842, a regular line of day and night steamers stopped at Tivoli. With the opening of the Hudson River Railroad in 1851, Tivoli became a principle wood and water station for the steam locomotives, providing employment for 150 men from the village.[56] Related industries sprung up. The railroad led to increased business on the Saugerties/Tivoli passenger ferry, where daily connections with every train became a strong selling point for passengers traveling on to the west. The steam ferry,

Tivoli Landing: This early 19th century engraving taken from a Federal Navigation Handbook *in 1880, shows the busy landing built up on the river before the railroad arrived in 1851. Steamboats and sloops operated on the river into the mid-1800s, to deliver and load goods for transport between New York and Albany.* Rokeby Collection.

The Air Line, became a legend in Tivoli, running daily between Tivoli and Saugerties for more than 50 years, between 1860 and 1915. Ferry service finally ended in Tivoli in 1940 after two centuries of almost continuous service between Tivoli and Saugerties.

The riverside village had its share of entrepeneurs in the 1900s. James Outwater, a mid-century freighter at the landing also built a hotel, ran the steam ferry *Chelsea* and operated a shad and fishing business that employed 46 men with a payroll of $1,380 a month.[57] Palmer Cook operated a milling business at the falls on the White Clay Kill for nearly 50 years. In 1820, his mill processed 1,500 pounds of wool, operating one carding machine and five looms, employing five men, with sales of cloth valued at $2,000. In 1860 his production used

The Airline: *This single bow steam ferry, with only one pilot house at the bow, made the Tivoli-Saugerties run for over 50 years. Because of her peculiar design, the boat had to be turned at each landing in order for the bow to be in front.* Losee Collection.

twice as much wool and, using three looms, three carding machines and 150 spindles, employing four men, he produced $3,200 worth of cloth. Cook retired by 1870, a rich 82-year old with a personal fortune of $5,000 and real estate worth $3,000. His occupation, listed in the census for that year: "gentleman."[58]

Tivoli Rail Road Station: Because there was no railroad on the west bank until later in the century, Tivoli became an important stop in mid-century for passengers continuing west. An overpass (left) north of the Tivoli station (right) allowed passengers disembarking from the train to safely cross the tracks and catch the Tivoli-Saugerties Ferry to the west. It was removed about 1900. Fred Briggs Collection.

Tivoli, at the river, and Madalin, at the upper crossroads, merged in 1872. Two years later they incorporated. The Reverend James Starr Clark, minister at St. Paul's Episcopal Church, and Tivoli's first president, made clear the priorities for the new village in his first board of trustees report: "Good order, good walks and the abatement of offenses to public health and morals."[59]

Tivoli's population reached its peak in 1890, at 1,350 people. It declined to half that number in the 1970s, after its railway station was demolished. Finally in 1990, 100 years after its heyday, the village population once again reached over 1,000.

Four Corners at Tivoli: A turn of the century street scene shows Broadway, looking west, in the old village of Madalin (upper left). The south side shot of Broadway (upper right) shows more clearly the store that today is Gary DiMauro's Real Estate. What appears to be a livery stable was taken down to build the Hotel Morey (lower left). The tavern eventually moved across the street, where, after several changes of name, the longstanding business still remains as Morey's. C.H. Moore built this large commercial brick building shown, c. 1920 on the corner of Broadway and North Road in 1899 (lower right). Tivoli Archives and Fred Briggs Collection.

Chapter 15
The Four Corners of Red Hook

a devastating fire on Prince Street in April of 1894 promoted the incorporation of the Village of Red Hook. Whipped on by a heavy southeasterly wind, it destroyed four houses, damaged several other, as well as several barns, stables and a livery stable, before volunteers managed to check it through an old-fashioned bucket brigade. It was just about out by the time the horse drawn hand-pumper, The Pocahontas, arrived from Rhinebeck, and the DePeyster Hose Company from Tivoli.

East Market Street: Cars began to appear along Red Hook's unpaved roads about the same time electricity poles were first strung. The Conklin and Allendorf block can be seen on the left. Down the street is the unusual three-story metal building, the Curtis Hardware Store. It became Stockenberg's in the 1920s and remains a hardware store today. EBHSRH Archives.

West Market Street: Looking west, the original Road to the Lower Landing, was lined with these maples, which shaded teams like the one pictured, until they were all taken down to widen Market Street in the 1940s. The old hotel is on the left, the Gedney Block on the right. Electricity has not yet been strung along the dirt roads. EBHSRH Archives.

South Broadway: The Massoneau Building (left) and the Tobacco Factory with its bell tower can clearly be seen in this c. 1906 photograph. The Red Hook Hotel is on the right. EBHSRH Archives.

North Broadway, c. 1915: Automobiles replaced horse and wagons on village streets by the 1920s and the first gas pumps appeared. The first Chevrolet dealership was in the Scism Building, (right) built around 1927. Cars were sold and serviced right in front of the dealership, until the 1950s. EBHSRH Archives.

The fire so shook the village—which with a population of 900 had now grown to almost twice the size of Upper Red Hook—that some four months later its residents voted to incorporate and create a water district. Tivoli had incorporated 20 years before for sidewalks; Red Hook did it now because it needed its own public water supply and fire company. The first firehouse was planned the same year, 1894, on Prince Street—on the site of the worst of the fire.

West Market Street Today: The B.F. Gedney building on the northwest corner of the Broadway and West Market Street has housed a drug store since around 1900. Photo by Douglas Baz.

East Market Street Today: On the north side, the Conklin and Allendorf block houses offices, small shops and apartments, and a delicatessen.It housed Aucock's Market for over 30 years in the 20th century. Photo by Douglas Baz.

The Southwest Corner of Market and South Broadway: The old Red Hook Hotel was torn down in 1963 to make way for a gas station. Today there is a gas station and convenience store. Photo by Douglas Baz.

The Southeast Corner of Market and South Broadway: A bookstore occupies the old Massonneau Building. The Scism Building next door is now a jeweler and newspaper office. The Tobacco Factory (far right) now houses a health food store. Photo by Douglas Baz.

The tobacco manufacturers were the first to build at what would become the commercial center of the town—the Four Corners in the village. In 1812 Claudius Massonneau bought out a lease he had with John Armstrong, and built a store at the corner of East Market Street and Broadway. In 1855, he replaced the store with a three-story Italian Renaissance Revival brick building, which makes up one of three handsome, commercial brick three-story buildings that still dominate the Four Corners in the village. Massonneau's served as a gathering place for town meetings. It housed the first public library in 1899. Teams of horses passed under an arched entryway to a public shed, in a later addition built behind the building in the 1860s.

The Massonneau Store c. 1895: A team of horses could easily drive through the stable entrance built in the wooden extension behind the brick Massoneau building (1855). The annex housed the town's first public library. Losee Collection.

The Four Corners

The large Aucock block, with its variegated slate roof, first called the Conklin and Allendorf building, went up across from the Massonneau Building in 1879. Merchants Conklin and Allendorf operated a general store there. A three-story brick addition was added later, and housed the Coon and Hoffman Shoe Store, and Hutton's Drug Store. The Aucock family ran their grocery store there for 50 years, before selling it in the 1960s.

Two other impressive brick buildings, with slated mansard roofs, were built in the 1860s—the Gedney building and the Near and Burnett building—completing the three-story commercial blocks at the corners. Benjamin Franklin Gedney constructed his brick building in 1876 on the site of the old J. Seimon farm, an 18th century Beekman freehold. The old farmhouse is still attached to the commercial block. Gedney ran a drygoods store in the building for decades and leased five additional shops in a brick addition on West Market Street. It has housed a drug store for nearly 100 years. A small two-story brick building just west of the Gedney building was the site of one of the earliest Red Hook Post Offices. It now serves as a restaurant.

A Young Man Poses: Benjamin Franklin Gedney built this long brick commercial extension to his fine, three-story brick building around the time of the Civil War. Until the 1950s, when they were covered over with sidewalks, there were several steep basement entrances, like the one shown in this c. 1890 photo. Losee Collection.

"Going Upstreet:" Children lounge in front of an early Red Hook Post Office, next to the Near and Burnett Building (seen in the photo on the left) around 1900. The colloquialism, "going upstreet," was a common expression until the 1960s, as was "going crosslots," taking a short cut across the numerous, large backyards. Fred Briggs Collection.

The adjacent Near and Burnett building, constructed by an enterprising local carpenter, Daniel Van DeBogart, housed, at different times, a pool hall, a bakery and a furniture store. But perhaps it was best known as housing the local undertaker, John Burnett, who advertised his furniture and coffin-making, along with his undertaking services, as an original two-for-one proposition.

The First National Bank of Red Hook was founded in 1865 by William Chamberlain, and built on the corner of Prince Street and North Broadway, where it served the community for the next 100 years. The building is now the village hall; the bank has evolved into Key Bank, located since the 1960s on West Market Street.

Stately Homes Appear with Prosperity

By the end of the century, Red Hook began to look more like the prosperous village it was becoming. Some elegant homes were constructed, especially along north and south Broadway, as the village prospered. The Massonneau, Nicks and Hendricks families, who at one time or another were partners in the tobacco business down the street, built their homes south of the tobacco factory. The Nicks' home served as the town's firehouse in the 1950s and 60s. It became Firehouse Plaza in the 1980s. The Red Hook Inn was built for

The Town Band: Musicians gather for an open air concert about 1885 on the porch of Hendricks House, later Dr. Traver's home, the Regis Hotel and, now, the Red Hook Inn. Alise Norton Collection.

Jeremiah Hendricks, eventually becoming the home of a local physician, Dr. Traver. For many years the Inn had a beautiful sunken garden to the south, surrounded by a black wrought iron fence. Each Christmas season the village decorated a 40-foot spruce tree on the edge of the garden with lights that could be seen throughout the village. The house became a tavern, operating in the 1940s and 50s as the Regis Hotel. Musicians gathered there to play for concerts and dances.

The garden was filled in, in the 1940s to make way for a gas station; the an insurance office occupies the site today.

The Hendricks Family Gather At Their South Broadway House c. 1880: This unusual octagonal home was built by Tobacco Factory partner Allen B. Hendricks in 1864. It is now the Red Hook Public Library. EBHSRH Archives.

Sunken Garden: Dr. Traver's beautiful gardens, surrounded by a wrought iron fence, graced South Broadway north of the library. They were tended by a special gardner, seen in this early photo. EBHSRH Archives.

The Allen B. Hendricks place, the landmark octagonal building, inspired by the theory and design of phrenologist/philosopher Orson Fowler, became the home of the Red Hook Public Library in the 1930s. Across the street, the Massonneau family built a handsome clapboard house, which for 50 years was the home of the late Dr. Frederick Zipser and his wife, Ruth.

Citizens Band: Attending a firemen's parade around the turn of the century, Red Hook's Citzens Band poses on West Market Street in Rhinebeck. The old Rhinebeck firehouse is on the far left. Pat and William Asher Collection.

Mapleton: *Jacob Elseffer lived and practiced law at this fine house surrounded by gardens on North Broadway. Torn down in the late 1950s to build the A&P Supermarket, it is now the site of the a pharmacy. Losee Collection.*

Further south on Broadway, General Armstrong built *Wayside,* an elegant house, with spacious grounds that covered most of the southwest quadrant of the village. He built his village home about 1840, with his son, Colonel Henry B. Armstrong, after moving from *Rokeby,* which he sold to his daughter and her husband, William B. Astor.

Mapleton, a handsome house surrounded by gardens running through to Graves Street, was located north of the Aucock block, and was the home of attorney Jacob Elseffer.

Street Scene: *Gas lamps and white picket fences lined many streets before roads were widened and electricity hung on poles. Here the George Hart family poses for an early stereoptic photograph taken around 1875 in front of their house on East Market at the corner of Graves Street.* Alise Norton. Collection.

Wayside: *Built by John and Henry Armstrong after they sold* Rokeby, *the house was demolished in the 1920s to build St. Christopher's Roman Catholic Church. Part of the Armstrong estate became the site of the old chicken pie factory, then Perx Products, on South Broadway.* EBHSRH Archives.

Dr. Robert Carroll: *The local physician who cared for Red Hook residents in the last half of the 19th century poses in his horse and carriage for this 1874 stereoptic taken in front of his house at the northeast corner of Linden Avenue and West Market Street.* Rokeby Collection.

J.W. Hoffman House: *Built as a private residence by the family that owned the Tobacco Company in the mid-1800s, it was later the Hoffman Inn boarding house. In 1937 when the local high school burned, it became a temporary school. It is now a bed and breakfast.* Alise Norton Collection.

Mansion row, an elegant string of homes along the original Post Road, still stands across from the Village Memorial Park north of the Elmendorph Inn. The three-story clapboard *Hoffman House* was built in the 1800s as the residence of the Hoffman family, who at one time owned the tobacco factory in the village. It has a mansard roof and iron cresting. To the south, and set back from the road, is a smaller building, which housed their servants and was a carriage house. The *Hoffman House* served as a public high school for several years while the brick central school was being built on Linden Avenue. Today it is

Massonneau House: *Built on South Broadway by the owners of the Tobacco Factory, this elegant Victorian was razed in the early 20th century. It is now the site of a funeral home.* EBHSRH Archives.

Robert B. Hevenor House, 1874: One of several Victorians that dominate the Old Post Road on "Mansion Row," this striking and colorful house is known as the Painted Lady. Rokeby Collection.

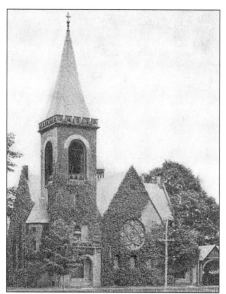

St. Paul's Lutheran Church: The Lutheran church on South Broadway, with its large cemetery, commands the largest greenspace in the village. Over 1,000 people attended the laing of the cornerstone at the new church in 1894. The original German Reformed congregation dates back to 1714, when it was estableished in Rhinebeck. Fred Briggs Collection.

a bed and breakfast. Just north of Hoffman House is the *Painted Lady,* a stately Victorian painted in multiple period colors.

Village Churches

The first church to be built in the village, St. Paul's Lutheran Church, was established by a German Reformed congregation soon after the Armstrong development. In 1796, the congregation bought five acres of land for 30 pounds from John Armstrong in Red Hook and moved to the lower Red Hook Village from Pinck's Corners a few miles south. The new church's original German Reformed congregation dates back to 1715, when it was one of two German congregations of Palatines that settled at Pinck's Corners near the corner of Route 9 and 9G. The two congregations, who shared a single wooden church, split in 1730. The Reformed stayed at the small log church at the corner until 1796, and the Lutheran congregation built St. Peter's Evangelical Lutheran Church (now called the Old Stone Church.) just down the road. The small cemetery at the corner of routes 9 and 9G is a reminder of the site of the original church.

The present church, built in 1890, replaced an original frame church and its successor, an 1834 stone church. Services were delivered in German only until 1823. In 1846, the congregation joined the Lutheran Synod and the church was renamed St. Paul's Evangelical Lutheran Church of Red Hook.

The town's Methodists first congregated at the 18th century Peter Dodd house, once the home of Mrs. Christina Moul, which stands adjacent to the Lutheran church. Methodist circuit riders stopped at the "Red Hook Mission," beginning in 1827. Fancher's Hall, another early site of worship, was located on Graves Street. In 1848, Mrs. Edward Livingston of Montgomery Place and William Chamberlain of Maizefield, commissioned the architect A.J. Davis to design a new church for the Methodists on property donated by Phillip Gilbert Fraleigh at the corner of West Market and Church streets.

Richard Upjohn, the pre-eminent designer of churches in his day, was architect of the Gothic Revival-style Christ Episcopal Church, built by the Astors on Armstrong land in 1855 across from St. Paul's. Christ Church, too, like the Lutheran Church was established as a result of a falling out among a congregation—this time the congregation of St. Paul's Episcopal Church in Tivoli.

Beginning in the 1840s with the development of the railroad, many Irish began to move to town, emigrating, as well as moving from New York City. As the Irish-Catholic population increased and families established farms, found jobs on the railroad and the fledgling telegraph industry, as well as service jobs on the local estates, the need for Roman Catholic services increased. St. Christopher's Roman Catholic Church was built in the village in 1925, to supplement the services held at St. Sylvia's in Tivoli and the Church of the Sacred Heart in Barrytown. This Gothic-style stone church was erected immediately north of John Armstrong's *Wayside*, which burned in the early 1920s.

Christ Episcopal Church and Parsonage: The Gothic Revival church was designed by the noted ecclesiastical architect, Richard Upjohn, and built in 1855 by the Livingston/Astor family of Rokeby. The rectory was completed in 1861, just before this photograph was taken on December 9, 1862. This Astor family picture, the earliest known photograph of the village, shows the open, plain landscape of the village in mid-century. The fields of the Gilbert G. Fraleigh farm, in the background, dominated the southwest quadrant of the village, and Fraleigh, Phillip, Garden and Church streets were not yet developed. Rokeby Collection.

The Lutheran and Episcopal churches (and much later in the 20th century, the Catholic Church) built attractive parish houses, rectories and the large park-like Lutheran cemetery. These buildings and grounds form a group on both sides of Route 9, at the southern gateway to the village, creating one of the most significant features of the village.

St. Christopher's Roman Catholic Church: Built in 1925 on the site of the old Armstrong house, Wayside, the European Gothic style church is considered the finest stone masonry construction in the village. Photo by Len Vogler.

Chapter 16
Twentieth Century

While the late 1800s saw a consistent increase in the population of Red Hook Township and its two villages, the turn of the new century signaled a decline. From a peak of 4,471 people in 1880, the census fell to 3,400 by 1940, then only rose to 4,200 people over the next decade. Farming, especially dairy farming and the diversified small family farm, began its long decline, a situation made worse by the Depression years. Young men looked to the cities to find work and to support their families. It was in Poughkeepsie, 20 miles to the south, where most of the county's growth concentrated in the first half of this century.

Apple Picking: Long skirts did not deter women from pitching in at harvest time. This shot was taken in the early 1900s at the Losee Farm in Upper Red Hook. Farms were still diversified, but about that time emphasis was on the increasingly profitable fruit production. Losee Collection.

Going to Market: Apples, packed in barrels and loaded ready to go. Trucks began to appear on the farm in the 1920s. G. Gordon Mead of Upper Red Hook had the first truck around. "It was an open-cab, crank-start, with no doors or roof, and it went about 15 miles per hour," his son Sydney Mead recalls. Before cold storage companies came to town about 1930, farmers caught the night train at Barrytown or Tivoli to ship apples to New York. Losee Collection.

However Red Hook took immediately to the new spirit of the 20th century. The first decade alone brought libraries, electricity, telephones, automobiles, moving pictures, and the biggest party to hit the town before or since.

Tractors and trucks came to the farm, as well as mechanized sprayers, milking machines and harvesters. Commercial fruit growing gained prominence and would continue to do so throughout the 20th century. Two cold storage houses were built with the onset of electricity, competing for the business of the new fruit packing industry and cider mills.

The Central New England Rail Road continued its run between Rhinecliff and Connecticut, supplying milk to the new Borden milk plant near the village depot, occupying the former Baker Chocolate factory. It then shipped the pasteurized bottled milk, as well as fruit from cold storage, to points east in New England and south to New York.

Grange

In the early 20th century the Grange Hall became the gathering place among Red Hook's farm families. John Fulton founded the Red Hook Grange in Upper Red Hook in

1902. Fulton's granddaughter, Harriet Norton, remembers Monday, Grange night, as the high point of the week.[60] Children became members at age 13, and accompanied their parents to weekly meetings, where there were lecturers, entertainments and, always, discussions about farm problems, legislation, crop prices and weather—everything related to agriculture. The highlight of the year was the Dutchess County Fair, where men, women and children displayed the best of their harvest and husbandry, competing for first prize in everything from livestock and poultry, to canned goods, vegetables and flowers.

Grange Hall. The Upper Red Hook Academy building served as the Red Hook Grange for 50 years. Farm families regularly gathered there for lectures, dinners and programs involving the entire family. EBHSRH Archives.

For 50 years the first Red Hook Grange was located in the fine, two-story Red Hook Academy building in Upper Red Hook. Lightning struck the building twice, in 1917 and in 1954. When it did not survive the subsequent fire, the Grange moved to the old firehouse on Prince Street in the lower village, where it remains. During this period, the Masonic Lodge, the Order of the Eastern Star and the Order of Elks were established, further enriching the life of the community. More recently, the Veterans of Foreign Wars post on Elizabeth Street has done the same.

The New Library

There was a progressive spirit in the air at the turn of the new century. Great interest was fostered in libraries, public education and self-improvement, especially in New York State. Both the Red Hook and the Tivoli public libraries were formed around 1898, when the state was funding half the cost of the public library projects. Red Hook's first library opened its doors with 850 volumes on the second floor of a building attached to the Massonneau Building at the Four Corners. The library board hired a part-time librarian for $40 a year, with the stipulation that he pay for the oil and fuel to heat and light the rooms. It later moved to the second floor of the Aucock building.

Red Hook Public Library: Purchased in 1935, the former Hendricks house is one of only a few octagon buildings in Dutchess County. The ten-room, three-story house was built of poured Rosendale cement and features a "blind" cupola. The clock once chimed the hours for the community, but has since disappeared. EBHSRH Archives.

An endowment, a gift from Libbie Benner Perrine and William Massonneau, led to the purchase, in 1935, of the present octagonal building on South Broadway from the A. B. Hendricks family, for $3,850.[61]

Politics Comes to Town

Some of the liveliest stories to come out of Red Hook as the town entered the new century had to do with politics. In 1896, the town hit the front page of "The New York Times," when presidential candidate William Jennings Bryan vacationed in Upper Red Hook. Bryan, a populist Democrat and renowned orator known best for challenging the gold standard in passionate campaign addresses, was running that year against William McKinley. He came with his wife to visit her old friend, Libbie Benner Perrine, the public library patroness whose family owned the local general store in Upper Red Hook. Each morning Bryan would hold a press conference on the steps of Perrine's store, with leagues of newspapermen planted outside to follow him throughout his day. His fishing trips to Spring Lake and speeches in Tivoli were each duly reported in the New York newspapers for over a week, dateline Upper Red Hook. It would be the only time Red Hook was datelined on the first page of "The New York Times," above the fold.[62]

Chanler Park and the "Monster Clambake"

A local man, however, generated the greatest political excitement of all. "Sheriff" Bob Chanler's run with politics in the first decade of the century captivated Dutchess County, and Red Hook in particular.

The Chanler Band and the Campaign of 1906: One of many local bands organized and supported by "Sheriff Bob" and his family, the local musicians (left) gathered at Chanler Park in Red Hook in the big campaign year of 1906. Robert Chanler and his brother, Lewis Stuyvesant Chanler, ran for office the year of the "monster clambake." Supporters (right) piled in a campaign car at the famous clambake, to garner votes. Chanler Park was in the area of the presentday Triebel's garage on South Broadway. Rokeby Collection.

One of the eight Chanler orphans, great-grandchildren of William B. Astor, Robert W. Chanler was raised at Rokeby, wealthy, impulsive and full of undirected energy. He was already recognized in New York and Paris as a decorative painter when he decided in 1901 to run for State Assembly from the Red Hook district. He set about making himself known to his electorate as only a Chanler could do.

First he bought a farm just south of the village and set aside 30 acres creating Chanler Park. It was located near today's Old Farm Road. Chanler had built a ballpark with bleachers and a race horse track (later it doubled as an airplane landing strip). He sponsored half a dozen baseball teams and brass bands throughout the county, equipping and outfitting them all with new "Chanler" uniforms. He put on picnics and races and games to the accompaniment of his brass bands, and to the delight of the local citizenry.[63]

In another winning stroke, Chanler imported a European prize bull to his Red Hook farm to improve Dutchess County farmers' stock, and offered its services free of charge. An imported, blooded stallion followed, on the same terms. Soon Dutchess farmers were winning the purses in stock competition with Ulster, its long-time rival. It came as no surprise when Chanler won his bid to represent the district in the New York State Assembly on his second try in 1903.

Chanler's most famous run was for Dutchess County Sheriff in 1906, when he shared the Democratic ticket with his brother, Lewis Stuyvesant Chanler. Lewis was the supervisor of Red Hook, and was running for Lieutenant Governor. Chanler Park was lively that summer, with local residents treated to the sight of Lewis Chanler campaigning by motor car, the first time an automobile had been used in a New York political campaign. The flamboyant "Sheriff Bob," campaigned in a horse-drawn buck board along the back roads of Red Hook, wearing western chaps and a cowboy hat.

On one of the hottest days of August, the Chanler brothers, Democrats in a heavily Republican county, staged what "The New York Times" reporter coined, "Mr. Chanler's monster clambake."[64] After a morning parade of fire rigs and companies, drum corps and brass bands, some 3,000 people gathered in shifts of 500 each beneath a "mammoth" tent to consume 65,000 clams, 2,000 bluefish, 80 barrels of sweet potatoes, 1,200 pounds of chicken, 1,800 lobsters, 6,000 ears of corn, 800 loaves of bread, 300 pounds of butter, 3,000 bottles of beer, and 5,000 cigars.[65]

To top off the day, the Chanler baseball team accommodated the crowds by beating its rival, Chatham. Guests didn't leave until after 5 p.m., wrote "The Poughkeepsie Journal" reporter, "each one with a warm spot in his heart for Robert W. Chanler."[66] Not surprisingly the Chanlers won both their races that fall, although in 1908 Lewis Chanler was defeated in his bid to become governor of New York.

The Monster Clambake: Over 3,000 people were fed at the huge barbecue and clambake given at Chanler Park in August of 1906. Here, hanging sides of beef are readied for the barbecue. Rokeby Collection.

Cheering the Home Team: Hundreds gathered that day in the stands at Chanler Park to witness the parade and ball game at the famous campaign clambake of 1906. Rokeby Collection.

SATURDAY, JUNE 24th, 1911
OLD HOME DAY
At Red Hook, N.Y.

Festivities will be held at

R. W. CHANLER'S PLEASURE PARK
SOUTH OF THE VILLAGE

AMUSEMENT CONTINUOUS THROUGHOUT THE DAY
Base Ball, Basket Ball, Athletic Contests, Roman Riding, Lassoing, etc. Automobile Parade

SPECIAL FEATURES
HORSE SHOW, HACKENEYS, POLO PONIES, Etc.
J. J. CHAPMAM. ....WARREN.DeLANO.
Cl .....ttee

A Gentleman's Trotting Contest   Large List of Entries.

ADMISSION ——— 25 CENTS

Home Town Gatherings: Many special events were held at Chanler Park, like this community day advertised in a 1911 poster. Losee Collection.

Telephones and Electricity

In 1905, the town board granted the first electricity franchise to a New Jersey man in return for supplying electricity for streetlights and other public venues.[67] In 1910, the first telephone poles and wires appeared on the still unpaved Red Hook streets, put there by John and Maurice Troy. The brothers founded the Hudson River Telephone and Telegraph Company in 1896, the predecessor to the Red Hook Telephone Company, which the Troys operated for more than 80 years.

Poles and Lines on South Broadway c. 1906: Electricity first appeared in Red Hook village, a little before the telephone and before the streets were paved. The large telegraph poles appeared years earlier. Outlying farms did not get electricity in some cases until the 1930s. EBHSRH Archives.

Troy's Telephone Company: This handsome Georgian brick building did not go up on North Broadway until the late 1930s, when crank-operated phones were replaced by the new dialing system. The house was built to house the new equipment. Photo by Douglas Baz.

On the first crank-operated phones, customers rang up the operator to tell her whom they wanted to reach. "You got to know most of the customers by voice, or number," recalled Red Hook resident Emma Coon, an operator at the phone company's offices over the Red Hook Drug Store in the 1930s. "It was a very small town."[68]

Short identification numbers, such as 72F, followed for each phone customer. The letter stood for the number of rings, for with party lines that contained as many as eight or ten families, it was important to know the individual sequences—one, two, long or short. Operators turned on the fire whistle each noon to announce the time.

The Troys built the three-story Georgian-style home on North Broadway to house the new dial service introduced about 1940. John Troy, who worked in the family business, remembers the first exchanges, because it was he who chose them: TUrner for Staatsburg, the first to get the service; TRinity for Rhinebeck; and PLateau for Red Hook, which is the origin of the current exchanges: 889 for Staatsburg, 876 for Rhinebeck, and 758 for Red Hook.[69]

The Movies

Modern popular culture made its first stand in the town by 1910, when Lyle Griffin built the first theater on East Market Street. The long-time manager of the W.H. Baker Chocolate Factory, Griffin operated the Lyceum Theater for many years. It functioned as a public hall, with basketball court and space for a dance hall on the second floor. The Lyceum hosted town meetings, high school graduations and the Chautauqua lecture circuit.

By 1915, however, it was silent films, with music provided from a small orchestra pit in front of the screen, that drew a big following. Winifred Herrick recalled, "If there was a Western playing, whenever there was a gun shot, I remember one of the fellas would hit the drum or the piano keys."[70]

The Fraleigh Store: The original building was built sometime in the 1870s or 1880s as a hardware store, run by Stickle and Ring. Phillip E. Fraleigh owned the store for many years, with a blacksmith and wheelright shop in the rear. Fraleigh Collection.

The Lyceum Movie House: Joseph Griffin renovated the Fraleigh Store and established the town's first moviehouse around 1910. It is now an antiques center. Photo by Douglas Baz.

Speed Limit: 10 mph

Red Hook's roads became busier with the development of the automobile, and residents had to face a new kind of menace. The automobile was a real intrusion to many citizens—noisy, unpredictable, and, above all, fast. In 1907, the residents of Annandale signed a petition asking that the town restrict the speed of these horseless carriages. That same year, the town responded by posting a 10-mile-per-hour limit. Agnes Losee Clark, the daughter of Dr. Edwin Losee, a respected physician who lived with his family in Upper Red Hook at the turn of the century, wrote about a confrontation with the new machine when on an outing in the family horse and buggy:

"Maudie (the horse) continued her same pace until an automobile wanted to overtake us and sounded its klaxon horn. Mother gasped and pulled on the reins to direct Maudie to the far side of the road, very near the ditch. I was frightened and tugged at the elastic band under my chin that held my straw hat to my head, and chewed it until Maudie was brought to an abrupt halt. Mother ... said, 'Be a good horse. Don't bolt, please don't bolt.' The old horse hadn't the faintest idea of bolting but tossed her mane indignantly. After being driven for years by Daddy, an excellent horseman, Maudie was well accustomed to the honks of various beasts known as automobiles.

Back onto the road we drove, into a cloud of dust left by the passing automobile."[71]

Despite the disruption, cars were here to stay. As if to signal the new era, in 1908 the great New York to Paris Automobile Race came through town, with the Albany Post Road as first leg of a 20,000-mile route. In 1909, many residents watched the spectacle of Glenn Curtiss and Orville Wright flying low, along the Hudson River, competing for a $10,000 purse in a race from Albany to New York. Both competitions coincided with the 100th anniversary of Fulton's introduction of the steamboat in this very valley. The high-speed age had arrived.

The Great War

Patriotism rang from the headlines of the "Red Hook Journal" in the spring of 1917, as the country entered World War I. "Our Country is at War!" boomed the April 13, 1917, headline. A "mass meeting of citizens" was called to be drilled in modern defensive warfare. By the time the U.S. decided to join in the European conflict, Red Hook had already known its first casualty. Young Victor Chapman of Barrytown, son of John Jay Chapman of Sylvania, and nephew of "Sheriff Bob" Chanler signed up to fight in France after graduating from Harvard in 1913. He was one of the first Americans to join the French when the war broke out in August, 1914, and he became the first American flyer to be killed in action—in a dogfight over France in 1916. He was 26 years old.

Chapman's death was big news in this country and in France, where he and Americans like him were revered for their sacrifice to the cause. In Red Hook, a "Victor Chapman" sewing circle was formed to aid the efforts in Europe.[72]

First Casualty: Victor Chapman at a Paris airfield just days before he was shot down over France in 1916. His head is wrapped in bandages from a recent injury (left). The Red Hook man was celebrated as the first American flyer to become a casualty of World War I. Private First Class Clarence W. Ham, of the 308th Field Hospital, 302nd Sanitary Train A.E.F. (right). The photo was taken in France in 1918 and sent back to his family in Red Hook. He came home from the war to work for the Gifford Company in Hudson, which made tools for cutting ice on the Hudson. Rokeby Collection and Maynard Ham Collection.

Citizens were urged to hang out their flags and to join the National Security League to learn to defend the country in an emergency. Ominously, a call went out for all "enemy aliens" to register at the Red Hook post office in July. All that summer, articles urged housewives to save fuel, to dry foods instead of canning, to economize. Shortages began to appear. By 1918, violet houses were closing for lack of coal. "Lay in wood, take no chances," warned an article in the "Tivoli Times."[73]

From the town of Red Hook, 154 traveled, in the common expression of the day, "over across" to fight in the war in Europe, most in the New York 77th Division. Thirty-nine of these were from the Village of Tivoli. Eight local soldiers died in the war.

The worst accident in the town's history was the derailment of a train carrying troops during World War I on the Tivoli North Bay causeway. Some soldiers were drowned. Since then, the short bridge over one of the inlets at the bay has been called "Soldiers Bridge." When the men came home in 1919, Red Hook pulled out the stops for the 60 returning soldiers. They were marched down the center of the village to the strains of the local community brass band. The Griffing Fire Company, the Boy Scouts, the Elks, the Victor Chapman local Red Cross chapter, and a long line of automobiles dressed out in red, white and blue bunting and filled with veterans of the Civil War, accompanied them. A huge celebration was held on the lawn of the Hoffman Inn, with speeches and visiting dignitaries. A clambake followed a special vaudeville show staged for their benefit. They were then treated to moving pictures at the Lyceum Theater, followed by a community dance.

Growing Violets: John Ham and Ed Decker working in Ham's violet house on Garden Street c. 1924. Red Hook shared the nickname, "violet capitol of the world" with Rhinebeck, and violet houses dotted the village in backyards and side streets. The delicate flower, so fashionable at the turn of the century, still grows wild throughout Red Hook. Maynard Ham Collection.

The 1920s

The 1920s were a time of great change, wrote the late John Losee, a local historian who with his wife Clara documented a great deal of Red Hook and Milan town history. Losee, who grew up in Upper Red Hook, had much to say about these times when horse and buggy operated alongside the new automobile on country roads and threshing and hay harvest were still shared tasks on the farms. Bicycles were a major mode of transportation, unless you could catch a ride on the Hucklebush into town.

Violet-growing was a big industry and Red Hook shared the title "Violet Capitol of America" with Rhinebeck. Corsages of delicate native or sweet violets were produced all over town for shipment by train to New York City and abroad. The evidence of the violet growing years can still be seen in the remnants of old green houses in many backyards, and in the profusion of violets that sprout in the nooks and crannies of village gardens each spring.

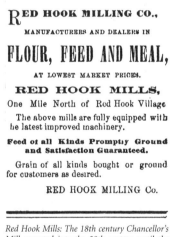

RED HOOK MILLING CO.,

MANUFACTURERS AND DEALERS IN

FLOUR, FEED AND MEAL,

AT LOWEST MARKET PRICES.

RED HOOK MILLS,

One Mile North of Red Hook Village

The above mills are fully equipped with he latest improved machinery.

Feed of all Kinds Promptly Ground and Satisfaction Guaranteed.

Grain of all kinds bought or ground for customers as desired.

RED HOOK MILLING Co.

Red Hook Mills: The 18th century Chancellor's Mill operated into the 20th century until the 1930s, providing farmers with grain and feed for livestock, ground plaster and cut tobacco for the local factory to package and create their cigars. This ad for the Red Hook Milling Company is from the "Red Hook Journal," 1901. Maynard Ham Collection.

Ice was harvested in winter from the millpond and delivered locally by the Red Hook Mill, which was still operating. The local markets would send their butcher to outlying farms weekly to choose the beef, pork and lamb that would be butchered and offered for sale to their customers within a day. Milk was 10 cents per quart, and a loaf of bread, 9 cents; sirloin steak was 50 cents per pound, and a Model A Ford cost less than $500.

Mill Pond: From an old family album, this pastoral scene, with the Red Hook Mill in the background, shows the Fraleigh family taking a leisurely paddle at the mill pond on Mill Road, one summer day around 1895. The pond was often used by local people for fishing and swimming. Fraleigh Collection.

Nine students graduated from Red Hook High School in 1924. Many young men and women in the 1920s still returned to the family farm as teenagers to work; higher education beyond age 16 was not yet the norm. For those who stayed in high school, it was expected they would take only the New York State Regents exams to earn their diploma. In 1920, four years of Latin and Greek were still offered to high school students.[74]

The "Roaring Twenties" did not bypass Red Hook. This was the era of the "native industries," as they were euphemistically called in the years of Prohibition. Hard cider and applejack, byproducts of the extensive orchards in town, were produced in unobtrusive spots and private stills throughout the countryside. Legitimate cider mills—there were at least five in town—often had their own "private" offerings in the backyard. Henry V. Shaw's Upper Red Hook Tea Gardens, a draw for the emerging tourist industry, was known for its private offerings, and became very popular during those years.

Replacing the Horse and Wagon: Oliver "Ollie" Rider, who would later become mayor of the village, shows off his newly acquired automobile sometime in the early 1900s, in front of the Red Hook Hotel. Driving machines began to replace horses before World War I, making the country more accessible. Maynard Ham Collection.

Shaw's Tea Gardens: During prohibition, visitors would drive to Red Hook in their fashionable new automobiles, taking advantage of the fresh air and the fresh applejack produced at roadside "tea" stands like this one in Upper Red Hook. The special "tea" was always available, somewhere in a back room, upon request. It is now the site of a motel. Fred Briggs Collection.

Enjoying the Country

Since the development of the railroad, Red Hook farms had been a draw for families from the city wishing to find fresh air, fresh food and sunshine. Beginning in the 1880 and 1890s, farmers' wives began operating boarding houses in summer for people who wanted to escape the city and enjoy the fresh air and countryside that Red Hook offered.

"Summer boarders evidently enjoy the beauties and healthfulness of this Locality," announced one item in the "Red Hook Journal" in 1899, " judging from the number that are almost daily arriving in this vicinity."[75]

Enjoying the Country c. 1915: Spring Lake, on the northeast boundary of Red Hook, was a popular destination for picnickers, (left) swimmers and vacationers. In 1950, John Colburn established a gas station and small store on South Broadway, previously the Kingfisher Inn and Midway Gas, c. 1930 (right). The bungalows, rented to summer visitors and Taconic Parkway construction workers, became the Colburn Mobile Home Park. Losee Collection and Arnold Colburn Collection.

Vacation cabins were built in Spring Lake to accommodate summer visitors, who made the journey by train to the Cokertown station nearby. Locals swam and picnicked on its banks. The Spring Lake Lodge became part of a burgeoning nightlife in spring and summer. The popularity of the automobile further encouraged a tourism industry that would grow to become one of the major economic mainstays of the local economy at the end of the 20th century. Families regularly made the trip to picturesque Red Hook for "pick-your-own" fruits, vegetables and flowers in summer and cut-your-own Christmas trees in winter.

Taking Off As the Black Baron: The late Cole Palen put Red Hook on the map when he set up his Old Rhinebeck Aerodrome in 1951 in an old hayfield on Norton Road. The former World War II private bought six vintage planes from Roosevelt Field with his life savings of $1,500. The working museum—planes are fixed up and flown all summer—draws thousands of visitors each year. Richard King Collection.

Recreation became part of the vocabulary for the citizens of Red Hook in the 1920s. While the Edgewood Club, said to be the nation's oldest tennis club, was established on Tivoli's Woods Road in 1884, the Red Hook Country Club was organized in 1926 at Shook's Pond near the old Schuyler patent boundary line east of the village. The nearby Red Hook Golf Club followed in 1935. For sportsmen, the Red Hook Rod and Gun Club became a focus of activity, as did the Red Hook Boat Club at Barrytown for fishing and sailing. In 1951, Cole Palen, a World War II buck-private who had just spent his life savings, $1500, to buy six old World War I airplanes, established the now famous Old Rhinebeck Aerodrome in a cornfield off Norton Road. Famed for its flying performances, its antique planes have been rescued, restored and flown to the delight of thousands of visitors each summer season, for over 30 years. Palen died in 1993, but the aerodrome continues to operate.

For more than a century, in winter, the sport of iceboating, sometimes called hard water sailing, was enjoyed on the Hudson River and South Bay in Red Hook. They were once the province of the moneyed classes, who competed among themselves with their famous Hudson River stern steerers—iceboats with names like *The Icicle,* originally owned by the family of President Franklin Roosevelt of

Seeking the Black Ice: Two antique Hudson River stern steerers sail southward toward Rhinecliff at the end of a perfect day for iceboating. The Vixen, left, once owned by President Franklin Delano Roosevelt's family, now belongs to Reid Bielenberg of Germantown. The Rip Van Winkle is owned by the J. W. Aldrich family of Red Hook. Thomas Brener, Museum of Rhinebeck History, 1981.

Hyde Park, *The Jack Frost* and *The Rip Van Winkle.* In the 1880s, they raced their favorites in serious winter competitions each year from Hyde Park to Tivoli. In the last several decades, with the revival of the Hudson River Ice Yacht Club, the 19th century iceboats have been pulled from long storage in local barns, repaired, restored and, once more, have been launched from Barrytown and Tivoli, to sail the "black ice." This search for the perfect ice is "a mostly heart-breaking passion," admits Chris Kendall, owner of *The 999,* built in 1880. "You wait and wait for the ice, and you wait and wait for the wind, and once in a while it works, and it's all worth it."[76]

Improving the Roads

In 1918, the Village of Red Hook targeted $8,000 in its annual budget to pave the village streets. However, paving as we know it—a hard road surface—did not come to Red Hook until around 1930. The money put aside in 1918 was most likely for an oil and stone or gravel surface. The old Post Road was "improved" as state Route 9 in 1928 and the old lower village's Hardscrabble past was finally put behind it. Route 9G followed soon after, in 1936. By the late 1940s, the old road to Pine Plains east of Red Hook, State Route 199, was widened to handle traffic from the Taconic State Parkway.

Building the New Roads: A crew pauses from their work with a stone crusher c. 1919. The crushed stones were used as materials to surface town roads around World War I for the new automobile. Still, many country backroads were not paved until the 1950s. William Teator Collection.

The newly surfaced roads, built for the speedy automobile, bypassed the old hamlets of Barrytown, Annandale, Tivoli and Upper Red Hook, and went straight through Red Hook Village. This redrawing of the old travel patterns changed the look of the village while helping preserve the charm of Tivoli and the other 19th century hamlets.

The One-room Schoolhouse

Area resident Doris Lasher Tieder, who grew up on a farm on the border of Red Hook, wrote about the days of the one-room school house, which still played a major role in the Red Hook community of the early 20th century. From the time she was seven years old, she walked a mile to the Nevis school from her family farm, often passing her first teacher, Mr. Sheely, who boarded at a neighbor's home. Mr. Sheely routinely carried "a square, black lunch box under his arm… He unlocked the building, put up the flag, cleaned the slate board, and brought in the day's drinking water from the well next door. We all used the same long-handled cup to drink from…. At precisely nine o'clock, he pulled the rope for the school bell."[77]

The Nevis school was typical of the smaller district schools. There were 30 students between the ages of five and 20 years, in eight grades. The class in session sat on two long wooden benches at the front, while the others worked behind. Reading, spelling, penmanship, history, drawing and geography were taught in the seven-hour day. School was often dismissed in early spring so children could help with the planting on the farm.

Upper Red Hook District #6: The entire student body came out to have their picture taken in front of the public school on the Post Road in Upper Red Hook c. 1890. Built in 1879 by Robert Harris, the two-story structure with its fine decorative gingerbread molding, replaced an earlier one-room schoolhouse at the site, dating to 1829. In its heyday, the school served 40 students. The building still stands, however the siding is covered and the detail gone. Losee Collection.

There were no "snow days," Tieder recalled. "One of the men at our farm would hitch the horses to the sleigh, fill it with hay and give us a ride to school, gathering up all the cousins and friends along the way."[78]

Local schoolhouses were located in Tivoli on Broadway; in Red Hook Village on South Broadway; east of the Village on Route 199; in Upper Red Hook opposite St. John's Dutch Reformed Church; in Madalin on West Kerley's Corners road; in Barrytown west of the corners; and in Annandale (The first was at Bard Hall. It was replaced by a second, near the corner of Annandale Road and Route 9G.). The Nevis School, the Cokertown School, the Rock City School, the White

Returning Home: These Upper Red Hook youngsters, caught in the camera of Will Teator in the early part of the century, were returning home from school along the Post Road. The Mooney house is in the background. William Teator Collection.

School and Willow Glen School, all in adjoining Milan and Columbia County, also served Red Hook children, and eventually became part of the incorporated district in 1939.

Barrytown School Children: In 1881 the children from Red Hook School District #8 , Barrytown, gather with their teachers at Sylvania for a school pagent. The schoolhouse was on Barrytown Road. John Jay Chapman, owner of Sylvania, (far right) hosted what was probably an end-of-the-year celebration. Rokeby Collection.

District #7: Located just over the Milan town border, this Rock City school, with its small bell tower typical of most country schools of the day, was consolidated into the Red Hook Central School District in 1939. This early photo indicates why the school was called the Sand Bank Academy for many years. Losee Collection.

Students completing studies at the small district schools were eligible to attend high school. In 1905, District #4 in the village, called The Red Hook Union Free School, was renamed the Red Hook High School. The original two-story, four-room frame structure was expanded to serve the area high school students as well as the lower grades.

Public school transportation was not available until 1939 and high school students had to make their way to class in whatever way they could—by foot (the old "shanks mare," as it was called), by bicycle, on milk wagons going into town, on horse and buggy driven by parents or farm hands and sometimes by the Hucklebush, the old Central New England Railroad. Alise Cotter Norton, long time editor of the local "Red Hook Advertiser," grew up on a farm in Milan. She recalled boarding with a family in town during the winter months so as not to risk being stranded or late to school during snow storms and bad weather.

The Big Red Brick School

Red Hook Central School: Hailed as one of the finest new schools in the state, the new Red Hook school had all the latest educational features and equipment of the day, including labs, special kindergarten room and gymnasium/auditorium, when it opened in 1939. It consolidated ten country school districts that year, a move that was considered very progressive at the time. Ellen and James Hogan Collection.

When a fire destroyed the Red Hook High School in 1936, many in town saw it as an opportunity. After much debate, and several years of setting up high school classes at buildings around the village, a new school and consolidated district was planned. On the day of the decision "teachers and pupils with banners and placards, marched to the Methodist Chapel," where voters from eleven districts over-whelmingly approved the proposition, 866 to 117 votes.[79] Taking advantage of a Dutchess County neighbor in the White House, the town petitioned President Franklin Roosevelt and received help from his federal Works Progress Administration to build the new school on the old Maizefield property, right next to Van

Ness' 18th century mansion. The imposing red brick Georgian Colonial, which today still looks like it could have come from a Norman Rockwell painting, was praised as one of the finest schools in New York State.

All the little one-room schoolhouses closed their doors and turned over their records, with the exception of Tivoli. The outbreak of war in Europe prevented F.D.R. from making his planned appearance at the dedication ceremony on Sept. 6, 1939—a huge event preceded by parades, singing and speeches.

Tivoli Union Free School: Built in 1915 on the site of a simple frame school from the early 1800s, which was rebuilt and enlarged over the years, this handsome two-story public school served Tivoli children until the 1960s. When the town consolidated its small districts in 1939, Tivoli was the one exception. The school now houses apartments, and the old district is part of the Red Hook system. Tivoli Archives.

Until 1962, students from kindergarten through 12th grade went to school under one roof, and played on the surrounding ball fields directly in sight of David Van Ness' "blue mountains." When the children of the post-World War II "baby boom" began coming along in the early 1960s, space became so tight that the district, once again, had to farm out students to classrooms throughout the village. The Mill Road Elementary School was built north of the village in 1962 to solve the problem. The new high school followed a few years later, built just west of the 1939 building, which then became a middle school.

Highway Expansion Changes the Rural Scene

Rural life was changing in the small town of Red Hook. Where once all roads led to the landings and the upper and lower villages, now the main roads led to Poughkeepsie and New York or to Hudson and Albany, right through the Village of Red Hook. When the Taconic Parkway was constructed in the late 1940s, Red Hook Village again came on the map. For a while it was the northern terminus of the famous rural parkway built in the heyday of Franklin Roosevelt's Works Progress Administration. The plan was for travelers to exit the Taconic at Lafayetteville near Rock City, and drive west through the Red Hook, in order to proceed northerly to Albany by way of the Post Road or the Rip Van Winkle Bridge. This led to the widening of Route 199, and to the cutting of scores of century old trees that lined east and West

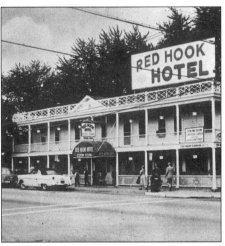

Business Revival: The Red Hook Hotel in the late 1940s or early 1950s, was modernized and set for the commuter age after the Taconic Parkway was built in the 1940s. Billboards on the way to town advertised the Elbow Room, a bar and restaurant that catered to travelers and became quite well-known between New York and Albany. Robert Rockefeller Collection.

Market streets. Businesses like the old Red Hook Hotel enjoyed a revival of sorts. The Elbow Room at the hotel became a landmark stop for travelers passing through Red Hook, and for locals as well. Gas stations began to spring up next to cow fields, joining the ranks of the new automobile repair and dealerships that had started to appear just before the war. Stanton Tremper, a Ford dealer, had one of the first car sales and repair businesses in town. Colburn's gas station just south of the village combined a country store, gas pumps and a long row of tourist cabins. The cabins later evolved into the Colburn Mobile Home Park.

Street Scene 1936: Young Lawrence Hogan holding out his cast, acquired from a recent accident, poses with his three-year old brother, Jimmy on North Broadway. The flat, concrete, uncompleted foundation for the new Telephone Company on the left. The Elseffer house stands where the CVS Pharmacy is today. Triebel's garage is in the background on the right. James and Ellen Hogan Collection.

The freighting business at the railroad stations in Red Hook Village and at Barrytown and Tivoli floundered in the wake of the faster, more convenient and more mobile trucks. The Taconic Parkway and, years later, the New York State Thruway made it easier to travel to New York City by automobile. The consequent competition forced the railroad to discontinue passenger and freight service to Barrytown and Tivoli in the 1960s, and raze the stations. With the cost of gasoline before World War II as low as seven gallons for a dollar, automobiles began to replace railroad cars for transportation. For those with a need to economize, the Twilight Bus Line operated a service in the 1940s and 1950s between its terminus on St. John's Street in the Village of Red Hook and Poughkeepsie, where most residents went for major shopping trips and often to work.

Workers at Tremper's Garage: Employees at the North Broadway garage (left to right) Albert Gay, Cecil Schook, George Coon, Paul D. Smith, two unknown representatives of Thompson's Laundry in Kingston, and Oliver Bradley, pose for a photo in the late 1920s. Stan Tremper Jr. Collection.

Triebel's garage c. 1920: William F. Triebel built the town's first garage on North Broadway in 1917. The second floor rooms were rented to summer tourists. A show room and machine shop made spare parts. The business moved to South Broadway in 1951 where Donald Triebel and his son still operate. Fred Briggs Collection.

One Stop Shopping c. 1936: Daisy Bigay minds the store at Midway Gas on South Broadway. Before 7-11s and Convenience Corners, owners of gas stations got the idea of offering groceries and refreshment to customers stopping to gas up. Colburn Collection.

Lasher's Garage: The full service garage on Montgomery Street in Tivoli, was owned and operated by Harold and Emma Lasher for 54 years, until it closed in the 1970s. Tivoli Archives.

The major shift of business and jobs towards Poughkeepsie and points south began in the 1930s and continued in the 1940s when International Business Machines (IBM) first brought its large electrical technology business to southern Dutchess County. By 1950 only a few non-farm-related industries remained in Red Hook, among them, the Voorhis-Tiebout soap dispenser factory, the Orchard Hills "chicken pie factory," and the Red Hook Asbestos Company in Upper Red Hook.

World War II

Boys graduating from Red Hook High School in June of 1942, found their futures on hold, as many answered the call to war. The 1943 yearbook, "Hardscrabble," was dedicated to "all the men and women serving in the Armed Forces of the United States who have ever attended school in Red Hook," 151 names in all.[80] Town military records for World War II, Korean and Vietnam wars, unlike the meticulous records kept for the Civil War by J.W. DePeyster, are sketchy. "Red Hook Advertiser" newspaper accounts estimate about 300 men served in World War II from the Red Hook area; a memorial at Tivoli lists 122 more. It is not clear if some or all of those from Tivoli are included in the newspaper estimate for the town. Eighteen soldiers died in action from Red Hook, and seven from Tivoli. These are listed on the war memorial at the Red Hook Village Memorial Park on North Broadway, in Tivoli's Memorial Park. Also listed are three casualties in the Korean War, and four in the Vietnam War.

Voorhis-Tiebout Soap Factory: Gordon Voorhis and Frank Tiebout started this factory that assembled soap dispensers, and dried the powdered soap that filled them, from 1937 to the 1990s. It is now a hardware and paint store. EBHSRH Archives.

Orchard Hill/Perx: Mary Hogan (top left) is shown working near the assembly line at "the chicken pie" factory on North Broadway c. 1962. Begun by the late Frank Smithers in 1939, Orchard Hill Farms produced frozen dinners and chicken pot pies for several frozen dinner companies. Ellen and James Hogan Collection.

Taking the Bus c. 1940: The Twilight Bus Company, with a terminal on St. John's Street in the village, ran a passenger service daily between Poughkeepsie and Red Hook in the 1940s and 1950s. Maynard Ham Collection.

Central Hudson Garage: In the 1920s, the Red Hook Power and Light Company was part of the Central Hudson system. It is now the village parking lot. This barn on Prince Street served as a garage and repair shop. L. Keith Denegar Collection.

Chapter 17
IBM and Second Half of the Twentieth Century

*n the first 50 years of this century, Red Hook had grown by just 325 people. But in the decade between 1950 and 1960, it swelled by half, and lost one-third of its farms.

When IBM established its operations near Kingston in the 1950s, Red Hook was still a small farming town. In 1955, the population of fewer than 4,500 was the same as it had been in 1880 at the peak of its 19th century growth spurt. There were 141 farms in town, half again as many fruit and dairy farms as in Rhinebeck to the south.

Then, in 1956, three things happened: IBM expanded its operations from Poughkeepsie to Ulster County; a bridge was built spanning the Hudson between Kingston and Rhinebeck, but landing right at the Red Hook town border; and the Louise Wirehouse dairy farm on Middle Road, on the southern border of town, was sold to a builder from Long Island.

Kingston-Rhinecliff Bridge: The dramatic span that connected Ulster County with Red Hook and Rhinebeck in 1957 had a great effect on development in Red Hook, where a large number of residents started to commute to work and shopping in Kingston. Before that, Poughkeepsie, to the south, and Hudson, to the north had been the most accessible cities for work and business for 200 years. Photo by Len Vogler.

The Wirehouse sale started a trend. Around the same time, two more big farms were sold, the Monroe Fraleigh farm and portions of the C.J. Baxter place, both on Whalesback Road.

The stage was set for one of the biggest transformations Red Hook had seen since the development of the railroad. The expansion of IBM and the building of the bridge led directly to the creation of half a dozen new residential developments.

The Wirehouse farm turned into Forest Park, the Fraleigh farm into College Park. Linden Acres, Willow Park, Red Hook Estates and the Prudente development followed, all carved from farm land. In the developments alone, five hundred new homes were built in town between 1957 and 1960.

Newspaper ads urged families to take advantage of the easy commute to Poughkeepsie and Kingston and the town's "superb" schools. Developers tempted young couples to sign up for a mortgage for the new tract houses for only a few hundred dollars down. Red Hook's reputation had begun in 1939 when the town consolidated its schools well before neighboring towns like Rhinebeck. The reputation for good schools would last throughout the century.

The six new housing developments increased the town's 1955 population by 60 percent to 7,550 people. By 1968, two new schools and a new recreation park and pool had been built to accommodate the influx of children.[81]

College Park Ad: Developers, finding cheap farmland in Red Hook and a growing job market in the area, in the late 1950s, made buying into the new developments as easy as possible for young couples, and took advantage of the town's already established reputation for good schools. Clare O'Neill Carr Collection.

Saving "Rural Character"

The boom brought to town an immediate debate and turmoil. Despite the optimistic ads, Red Hook faced the question posed in many northeastern communities at the time: how to accommodate growth, and still retain some control over standards of water, roads and traffic. And for the first time the broader question could be heard: how could the town grow and still retain the rural character of its first 200 years. The town was facing problems that come, said long-time farmer and town councilman Robert Greig, "when too many pastures are put under houses, instead of corn."[82]

There was no zoning when the first developments went up. The only restrictions placed upon the new builders were the relatively mild regulations from the county health department. The 116 homes initially built in College Park were placed on lots of a quarter acre or less, on ground so wet in places it wouldn't even hold the metal septic tanks.

It took a long time before a zoning law was finally adopted in Red Hook. The feeling at the time was, "No one is going to tell me what to do with my land," recalled a veteran of the debates, Red Hook Village attorney William Walsh.[83]

In the last quarter century, the town adopted regulations for zoning, building, water quality and conservation of wetlands. The town also adopted a master plan for growth, completing a town-wide survey that showed overwhelming support for maintaining rural character, green space and agriculture. The villages established zoning and planning regulations of their own. However, pressure from continuing change often made zoning codes outdated before the ink was entirely dry. Red Hook set up a permanent committee to consider ongoing changes in its master plan and zoning regulations in the 1990s.

Historic Preservation and Conservation in Red Hook

Eleanor Roosevelt at Tivoli: The famous first lady, pictured here with local American Legion Commander Billy Brown at the Tivoli Memorial Day ceremonies in 1956, spend much of her childhood at her grandmother Hall's, at Oak Lawn in Tivoli. Tivoli Archives.

One of the more interesting phenomena to come out of the rapid growth of the last half of the century has been the movement toward conservation and historic preservation.

As farms and apple orchards disappeared before housing developments, and historic buildings were replaced by parking lots, townspeople sometimes did not realize what they were losing until it was too late. However, because Red Hook's wealthy citizenry had inadvertently protected the land for so long by holding on to their large riverside parcels, the town's shoreline had remained largely intact. In recognition of this relatively untouched landscape, significant architecture and the role its early citizens played in the nation's history, the town's riverfront became part of a district listed on the National Register of Historic Places. Hudson River Heritage (HRH), founded locally in 1974, sponsored the application. A few years later, HRH documented the entire riverside district, from Staatsburg north to Germantown and including the hamlets of Tivoli, Barrytown and Annandale. As a result, in 1990, the secretary of the interior designated Red Hook's shoreline district part of the new Hudson River National Historic Landmark District—the nation's largest.

Beginning in the early 1970s and inspired by the nation's first Earth Day and the Bi-Centennial, Red Hook citizens joined new movements and organizations set up to preserve farmland, green space, ecologically sensitive wetlands and shoreline, historic structures and some of the fine architecture still remaining. The number and extent of these efforts is impressive. The Hudson Valley has one of the largest concentrations of private not-for-profit preservation organizations in the country. Red Hook is in the center of this activity, as well as being the focus of a significant number of state and federal preservation efforts. The following list, which does not cover numerous private preservation efforts among the town's churches, schools and private homes, tells the story:

- Beginning in the 1960s, Margaret Livingston's home, *Clermont,* was restored as a state historic site and popular scenic park. The community organization, Friends of Clermont, was formed to support the programs at the site.

- In the 1970s, the state bought the former *Ward Manor* property on North Bay in Annandale to preserve it from development as a power plant site and so manage the unique habitat. In 1982 it established the Tivoli Bays National Estuarine Research Reserve to protect the bays and the wildlife and plants that flourished there in the shallow tidal waters of the Hudson. It is one of only 24 such reserves in the country: Hudsonia, a private not-for-profit consulting group based at Bard College on the river promotes conservation and preservation of rare plant and animal species.

- The Egbert Benson Historical Society of Red Hook was founded in 1976, the same year the community banded together to form Friends of Elmendorph, and save the historic tavern in the village.

- The aging *Montgomery Place* was bought by Historic Hudson Valley, restored and opened to the public in 1988.

- The Winnakee Land Trust, taking its name from a local Indian word meaning "good land," was set up to conserve scenic lands and open space in Red Hook, Rhinebeck and Hyde Park in 1990. It has already put hundreds of acres in Red Hook under conservation easement.

- Working with the county, state and local landowners, Scenic Hudson, a local preservation organization, has saved hundreds of acres of open space and prime farmland in the town by buying development rights. This has enabled farmers to continue to farm the land, while resisting the high prices offered by developers to cut up the land into building lots. This, in turn, will help preserve the scenic gateways to the village. Poets' Walk Park, one of the few areas of public access to the riverfront, was also created in 1994 through the efforts of Scenic Hudson and several private landowners.

- The town Trails Committee and Greenway Committee are working on bike and foot paths that will eventually connect Tivoli on the north to the parks near the Saw Kill in the Village of Red Hook. More paths are planned along the old Central New England Railroad spur near Spring Lake.

- The Red Hook Conservation Advisory Committee has completed wetland and stream bank overlay maps to protect the town's water resources. In the 1970s, with the cooperation of Bard College and the local Rod and Gun Club, it undertook an extensive cleanup and stream watch program that returned health to the stream and allowed trout to flourish in the Saw Kill for the first time in almost 20 years.

- The community was galvanized in 1975 when Consolidated Edison announced plans to build a nuclear power plant in Upper Red Hook to supply electricity to New York City. Citizens packed meetings at town hall and the local school auditoriums to protest a plan they felt threatened their town's rural peace and security. The water intake for the cooling towers was planned just north of Bard College. The town fought the plan for more than 10 years. When electricity needs lessened and the New York power plant tried to sell the land to the county for a county-wide landfill, the town and its citizens stepped up again to battle that plan in a series of lawsuits that were eventually decided in Red Hook's favor in the 1990s.

Stepping into the Future

IBM downsized in the early 1990s, laying off several thousand local employees in Northern Dutchess and Ulster County. But the area electronics and computer industry still remains a major employer. Local fruit and vegetable farmers have developed extensive pick-your-own operations and farm market stands that draw hundreds of customers each summer to Red Hook orchards. Several farms, which once supported dairy herds, now raise sheep and horses. In the year 2000, the last dairy farm in Red Hook, Irving Fraleigh's, sold its herd and shut down its doors after operating in Red Hook for more than 100 years. However, in 1998, his relative David Fraleigh and his family celebrated their 200th year of continuous farming at Rose Hill farm just a few miles away. Rose Hill is still going strong as an orchard and pick-your-own operation.

These agricultural enterprises, along with attractions such as Clermont, Montgomery Place, Poets' Walk Park, the new Kaatsban Dance Center in Tivoli, Red Hook's Old Rhinebeck Aerodrome, and Bard's performing arts programming, combine to offer the town the chance for a prosperity that does not threaten the community's environment or quality of life.

Gehry on the Hudson: Bard College is planning to open its new 100,000 square foot performing arts center in 2002. Renowned architect Frank Gehry has designed the world-class facility, which will include, beside the seat performance hall, a smaller teaching theater, both equipped for modern scene changing, sound and lighting. It will serve students in Bard's theater and dance programs during the school year. In summer, it will be the site of a full-scale public program of theater, dance and music, hosting visiting theater companies and musicians, and the annual Bard Music Festival. Photo provided by Bard College.

A major impact on the town's future is expected to be the new world-class Center for Performing Arts designed by architect Frank Gehry. It is scheduled for completion in 2002 and is expected to draw major performers and audiences to Red Hook.

People from Red Hook still commute to Poughkeepsie, Kingston and Albany for work, with a growing number commuting by train to New York City from nearby Rhinecliff station, or from the cheaper Metro-North station, which set up a terminal in Poughkeepsie in the 1980s.

A growing number of people work at home, communicating with offices around the country through computer technology. Although growth has never matched the intensity of the 1950s and 1960s, three of the six developments in town have nearly doubled their size, and the population of Red Hook and its villages at this turn of the century is approximately 10,400 people. Red Hook is now a "bedroom" community, a town within commuting distance of good jobs, with good homes and schools and a breath of country living.

Much has changed over the last two centuries. However, families like the Heermances, the Mohrs, the Van Nesses and the Livingstons, who built their homes more than 200 years ago in the valley "beneath the Blue Mountains," might very well recognize that impulse to preserve what is best in the town they founded.

NOTES

1. Taken from a letter written by David Van Ness to a friend, while traveling back to his home in Red Hook, about 1800.
2. James H. Smith, *History of Duchess County,* quoting from Hendrick Hudson's Journal of 1609 in the History of New Netherland, pg. 36.
3. The poem was quoted in a talk given at St. Stephen's College in 1895, by John Lewis, a prominent farmer and local historian in Annandale. He quotes Charles Sprague, a social commentator and poet who lived between 1791 to 1875, and who published essays, poems and newspaper articles in the popular press.
4. The Map of Rhinebeck prior to 1812 shows the breakdown of the original Schuyler's Patent in Red Hook, the lots and their six Dutch owners. It was published in E.M. Smith's *Documentary History of Rhinebeck,* 1881.
5. An original Beekman deed between Andreas France and patentee Henry Beekman and his partner, John Rutsen, signed Oct. 20, 1718. This was reprinted in Howard Morse's Historic Old Rhinebeck: Echoes of Two Centuries, published by the author in 1908. On this same day the first Red Hook settler is recorded as having signed a lease with Henry Beekman for a farmstead in Red Hook. It became part of the Red Hook lands of Margaret Beekman Livingston.
6. William McDermott. "The Livingstons' Colonial Land Policy: Personal Gain over Public Need", printed in *The Livingstons Legacy, Three centuries of American History,* 1987, Bard College, Dick Wiles, editor. pg. 18-21.
7. Staughton Lynd, *Class Conflict, Slavery and the United States Constitution,* (Bobbs Merrill Co. Inc., Indianapolis, Ind., 1967, pg. 66), quoted in Lorna Skaaren's "Barrytown, New York: A Brief Social History,", 1983, pg. 4.
8. *St. John's Low Dutch Reformed Church: 175th Anniversary, 1788-1963,* Walter V. Miller, 1963, pg. 22-23.
9. "Brief History of Cedar Hill and the Sawkill," a research paper by Jacquetta Haley, Historic Hudson Valley, pg. 3.
10. Alexander Thompson Map of Rhinebeck, 1797. A copy is at the Elmendorph Inn, EBHSRH Archives.
11. Howard Morse, *Historic Old Rhinebeck,* 1908. pg. 180.
12. Helen Reed Delaporte, Horse and Buggy Age of the Old Town, a transcription of Red Hook/Rhinebeck town records, 1932. Copy, Red Hook Public Library.
13. Letter from Robert Livingston to Alida, his wife, April 28, 1714, Livingston-Redmond Papers, originals at Franklin D. Roosevelt Library, Hyde Park, from Roberta Singer, "The Livingstons As Slave Owners, The "Peculiar" Institution of Livingston Manor and Clermont, The Livingston Legacy: Three Centuries of American History, pg.69, Hudson Valley Studies, Richard T. Wiles, editor, Bard College, 1986.
14. Michael E Groth, "The Struggle to Build an Independent African American Community in Dutchess County: 1790-1820," Hudson Valley Regional Review, Richard Wiles, editor, Vol 14, #2, September, 1997, pg. 35.
15. "The Role of Dutchess County During the American Revolution," a Dutchess County American Revolution Bicenntenial Project, Poughkeepsie, 1976.
16. Letter from General George Washington to Brigadier General James Clinton, May 14, 1781, thanking him for his letter of May 7, 1781, and for his action in sending flour from Red Hook, Writings of Washington.
17. James H. Smith, *History of Duchess County,* pg. 180.
18. Letter from Gen. George Washington to Major General Israel Putnam, Oct. 25, 1777, thanking him for his letter from Red Hook, "the first authentic intelligence I received of the affair…I have not received a single line from General Gates, Writings of George Washington.
19. John Watts DePeyster, in an article written for the New York Times, Sept. 30, 1877.
20. Letter from Egbert Benson to his client, Mary Elmendorph, March10, 1773, post dated "Red Hook,"manuscripts, New-York Historical Society, New York, NY.
21. Letter from Egbert Benson to his friend, David Van Schaack of Kinderhook, May 15, 1773, postdated Red Hook. Manuscripts, New-York Historical Society, New York, NY.
22. Ad placed in The New-York Packett, by Philip Jacobs of Rhinebeck Precinct on July 21, 1783, advertising the Elmendorph for sale. EBHSRH Archives.
23. Nancy V. Kelly, "Rhinebeck Transition in 1799," Hudson Valley Regional Review, Sept., 1989, Vol. 6, No. 2, pg. 82.
24. Willis, Nathaniel Parker, Letters From Idlewild, Letter V., Adams, Arthur G., The Hudson Through the Years, pg. 108.
25. Edward M. Smith, *Documentary History of Rhinebeck,* 1881, pg. 55.
26. Lorna Skaaren, "Barrytown: A Brief Social History," pg. 32.
27. Red Hook Town Board Minutes, April, 1813, manuscript, Red Hook Town Hall.
28. Letter from A. Eggleston to Mr, Isaac Bird, Yale College, New Haven, Conn., posted from Redhook (sic), on June 20, 1815. Maynard Ham, Collection, Red Hook.
29. Richard C. Wiles, *Tivoli Revisited: A Social History,* 1981, pg. 9.
30. Minutes of the Meeting of the Elmendorph School District #1, Nov. 13, 1819, reprinted in a pamphlet, "Dedication of the Red Hook Central School," 1939.
31. Ibid., Elmendorph District Minutes, April 3, 1815.
32. Pamphlet commemorating the Red Hook Academy, published in Upper Red Hook, 1920s, Collection of John and Clara Losee, Archives, Elmendorph Inn, Red Hook.
33. Quotes from the John Curtis Diary, copied manuscript, Losee Collection, Archives Room, Egbert Benson Historical Society of Red Hook, Elmendorph Inn, Red Hook.
34. Letter to the Red Hook Journal, E.R.Holt and comrades, Nov. 5, 1861, Clara and John Losee Collection, Archives, Egbert Benson Historical Society of Red Hook, Elmendorph Inn, Red Hook, N.Y.
35. Ibid, C.S.Wilber, Jan. 20, 1863.
36. Ibid, Anonymous, Nov. 6, 1862.
37. Reamer Kline, Education For *The Common Good: A History of Bard College, the First 100 Years, 1860-1960,* Bard College, Annandale-On-Hudson, 1982, pg. 20-22.

38. Souvenir Booklet – 90th Anniversary, The Free Church of St. John the Evangelist, 1964, in the church records at Barrytown.
39. Lorna Skaaren, "Barrytown: A Brief Social History," pg 51.
40. *American Railway Guide and Pocket Companion,* Curran Dinsmore & Co., New York, June 1853. The pamphlet was published monthly and contained the schedules for railways with their steamboat and stage line connections throughout the U.S.
41. Statistics for the section on Red Hook and Rhinebeck industry in the 19th century were taken from the "New York State Census of the Products of Industry," 1835, 1850, 1860, 1880 and1913, as well as from the "U.S. Government Products of Industry" reports and the "New York State Inspectors Report," in various years. Microfilm and documents are part of the collection of Professor Richard Wiles, Hudson Valley Studies, Bard College.
42. William S. Massonneau, "History of the Red Hook Tobacco Factory," manuscript, archives of the Red Hook Public Library.
43. William Massonneau, Ibid.
44. Burton Barker Coon *Fifty Years Ago – Rural Life from 1875,* pg. 11.
45. Yearly report, New York State Department of Agricultural Economics, NYS College of Agriculture, Cornell University, July, 1875.
46. Raymond Brenzel, "History of Red Hook Grange #918: 50th Anniversary," May 15, 1952.
47. Yearly report, New York State Department of Agricultural Economics, NYS College of Agriculture, Cornell University, 1954.
48. Cynthia Owen Philip, "Fall's Fairest Apple," About Town," Tivoli, Fall, 1998.
49. Coon, Ibid.
50. Ibid New York State Inspector's Report, 1898."
51 "New York State Census of Products of Industry, 1850," microfilm, collection of Professor Richard Wiles, Bard College Hudson Valley Studies Department.
52. "Annual Report, NYS Department of Parks and Markets," 1918.
53. Lorna Skaaren, "Barrytown: A Brief Social History," 1983, pg. 49.
54. Skaaren, Ibid.
55. Red Hook Journal, July 30, 1863.
56. Joan Navins, *Tivoli 1872–1972.*
57. "New York State Census of Products of Industry, 1850," microfilm, collection of Professor Richard Wiles, Bard College Hudson Valley Studies Department.
58. Richard Wiles, *Tivoli Revisited: A Social History,* 1981, pg. 13.
59. Richard Wiles, Ibid, pg 23.
60. Clare O'Neill Carr, "Red Hook Grange Celebrates 90 Years," Gazette Advertiser, April 12, 1983.
61. Minutes of the Board of the Red Hook Free Library, 1898 – 1945, archives, Red Hook Public Library.
62. New York Times, July 6, 1896.
63. Lately Thomas, *The Astor Orphans: A Pride of Lions,* Washington Park Press, Albany, N.Y., 1999, pg. 176.
64. New York Times, August 24, 1906.
65. Poughkeepsie New Yorker, "The Chanler Clambake," August 25, 1906.
66. New York Times Ibid.
67. Minutes of the Town Board of Red Hook, Sept., 1905.
68. Interview with Emma Coon, Red Hook, 1998.
69. Interview with John Troy, Red Hook, Feb. 6, 1998.
70. Interview with Winifred Herrick, Feb., 1998.
71. Agnes Clark, Dutchess Days, Fithian Press, Santa Barbara, California, 1996. Pg. 98.
72. Red Hook Journal, July 13, 1917.
73. Tivoli Times Journal, Jan. 11, 1918.
74. John Losee "Remembering the 1920s in Red Hook," manuscript, archives, John and Clara Losee Collection, Archives, Egbert Benson Historical Society of Red Hook, Elmendorph Inn, Red Hook.
75. Red Hook Journal, July 7, 1899, Collection of Maynard Ham, Red Hook.
76. Gazette Advertiser, February 4, 1983, Sportsman take to the Hudson, article by Clare O'Neill Carr.
77. Doris Tieder, "Remembering the One-Room School House," PennySaver, March 30, 1983. Yorktown Heights.
78. Tieder, Ibid.
79. The Gazette Advertiser, special edition, Sept. 13, 1939, entirely devoted to the upcoming dedication of the new school and the history of the country schoolhouses closing to form the new central schooldistrict. Egbert Benson Historical Society Archives.
80. Hardscrabble, 1943 edition, senior class yearbook. Emma Coons Collection.
81. Statistics in this chapter were taken from a series of articles that covered the dramatic change in Red Hook beginning in 1957, published in October, 1987 in the Gazette Advertiser and written by Clare O'Neill Carr. Clare O'Neill Carr Collection, EBHSRH Archives.
82. Interview with Robert Greig, Ibid.
83. Interview with William and Patsy Walsh, Ibid.

BIBLIOGRAPHY

Books and Articles

A Brief History of the Church of St. John the Evangelist, Barrytown, NY, 1874–1964, compiled for the 90th Anniversary, Barrytown, NY, The Free Church of St. John the Evangelist, 1964.

Agnes Clark. *Dutchess County Days,* Santa Barbara, CA, Fithian Press, 1996.

Aldrich, John Winthrop. "A Brief Account: Cruger's Island and Adjoining Uplands," Annandale, NY, The Hudson Valley Regional Review, Vol. I, March, 1978.

Anderson, Jean Bradley. *Carolinian On The Hudson,* Raleigh, NC, Historic Preservation Foundation of North Carolina, Inc., 1996.

Arthur G. Adams. *The Hudson Through The Years,* Westwood, NJ, L.P. Lind Publications, 1983.

Barry, Elise. "Town of Red Hook Survey of Architectural, Historical, Cultural and Natural Resources," Red Hook, NY, Hudson River Heritage and the Town of Red Hook Conservation Committee, 1995.

Brenzel, Raymond. "History of Red Hook Grange #918, as written for the 50th Anniversary," typed manuscript, Red Hook, NY, 1952.

"Baptismal Records of All Saints Chapel, Upper Red Hook, 1884–1924," archives, Christ Episcopal Church, Red Hook, NY.

Bassett, Edmund. *Reminiscences of Red Hook (A story of the Village),* a series of articles published in The Red Hook Advertiser beginning November, 1926 and compiled by John and Clara Losee, Red Hook, NY, Red Hook-Tivoli Bicentennial Committee, 1976.

Bassett, Edmund. *Reminiscences of Some of the Highways and Byways of Red Hook,* a series of articles published in The Red Hook Advertiser, between April 10 and October 9, 1930, Red Hook, NY, Red Hook-Tivoli Bicentennial Committee, 1976.

Bielitz, Rev. Walter J. *History of St. Paul's (Zion's) Evangelical Lutheran Church of Red Hook,* Red Hook, NY, St. Paul's Church, 1941.

Brandt, Clare. *An American Aristocracy: The Livingstons,* Garden City, NY, Doubleday & Company, 1986.

Carr, Clare O'Neill. *The Red Hook Public Library: A Brief History,* Red Hook, NY, Red Hook Library Centennial Committee, 1998.

———. "Developments That Changed Red Hook Forever: Rertracing the legacy of the pre-zoning era," The Gazette Advertiser, February 4, 1988.

Clark, Andrea and Donnelly. "Red Hook Historical Walking Tour," Mill Road School Fourth Grade History Department, Red Hook, NY, 1996.

Coon, Burrton Barker. *Fifty Years Ago: Rural Life from 1875,* a series of articles by a Milan native, published between 1920 and 1942 in The Rhinebeck Gazette, The Red Hook Advertiser and The Rural New Yorker, compiled by John and Clara Losee, Red Hook, NY, Red Hook-Tivoli Bicentennial Committee and Town of Milan, 1977.

Crowley, Richard and Aldrich, John Winthrop. "St. Margaret's Home, Red Hook," Dutchess County Historical Society Year Book, Vol.78, Poughkeepsie, NY, Duchess County Historical Society, 1993.

"Dedication Program of the Red Hook Central School District," Red Hook, NY, Red Hook Central School, 1939.

Downing, A.J. *Landscape Gardening and Rural Architecture,* Mineola, NY, Dover Publications, 1991(replica of the original, A Treatise on the Theory and Practice of Landscape Gardening, Adapted to North America; With a View to the Improvement of Country Residences, New York, NY, Orange Judd Agricultural Book Publisher, 1865.

"Dutchess County Directory," 1893-1896,"Poughkeepsie, NY, 1896 (excerpts prepared by Marlene Hejnal, 1997).

Fredriksen, Beatrice. *The Role of Dutchess County During The American Revolution,* Poughkeepsie, NY, Dutchess County American Revolution Bicentennial Commission, 1976.

Gazetteer of the State Of New York, Albany, NY, 1813, 1823, 1836, 1842, 1872.

Groth, Michael E. "The Stuggle to Build a Free African-American Community in Dutchess County, 1790-1820," Annandale, NY, The Hudson Valley Regional Review, Vol. 12, September 1997.

Haley, Jacquetta. "Brief History of Cedar Hill and the Sawkill," Annandale, NY, typed manuscript, Historic Hudson Valley, 1987.

Hejnal, Marlene. "Historical Overview of Red Hook United Methodist Church," Red Hook, NY, 1993, typed manuscript.

Hoffman, Eugene A. *Geneology of The Hoffman Family, 1657-1899,* Albany, New York, Dodd, Mead & Co., 1899.

Holt, Wythe & Nourse, David A. *Egbert Benson: First Chief Judge of the Second Circuit (1801-1802),* New York, NY Second Circuit Committee on the Bicentennial of the United States Constitution, 1987.

Kelly, Nancy V. "Rhinebeck: Transition in 1799," The Hudson Valley Regional Review, Vol. 6, Annandale,, NY, September, 1989.

Kim, Sung Bok. *Landord and Tenant in Colonial New York: Manorial Society 1664-1775,* University of North Carolina Press, 1978.

King, Richard. *The Skies Over Rhinebeck, A Pilot's Story,* State College, PA., Jostens, 1997.

Kline, Reamer. *Education For The Common Good: A History Of Bard College, The First 100 Years, 1860-1960,* Annandale, NY, Bard College, 1983.

Leonard, Roger M. *The Red Church,* Upper Red Hook, NY, Roger Leonard, 1990.

Lewis, John N. "Reminiscences of Annandale , A Lecture Delivered before the Faculty and Students of St. Stephen's College, Annandale, Feb. 12, 1895," Annandale, NY, John Lewis, 1909.

Lindner, Christopher. "Grouse Bluff: An Archaeological Introduction," The Hudson Valley Regional Review, Vol. 9, Annandale, NY, March, 1992.

Lindsley, James Elliot. *This Planted Vine: A Narrative History of the Episcopal Diocese of New York,* New York, NY, Harper and Row, 1984.

Massonneau, William. "The Red Hook Tobacco Factory," typed manuscript, Red Hook, NY, Red Hook Public Library, 1932.

McCraken, Henry Noble. *Blithe Dutchess: The Flowering of An American County from 1812,* New York, NY, Hastings House, 1958

"Minute Book of the Red Hook Society for the Detection and Apprehension of Horse Thieves, 1796–1837," manuscript, New York State Archives, Albany, NY, copy, Red Hook Historical Society.

Morse, James. *History Old Rhinebeck: Echoes of Two Centuries,* Rhinebeck, NY, James Morse, 1908

Navins, Joan. *Tivoli: 1872-1972,* Tivoli, NY, Tivoli Bicentennial Committee, 1972.

Philip, Cynthia Owen and Gray, Mary Washburn. *In Pursuit of Conviviality and Sport: The Edgewood Club of Tivoli, 1884-1984,* Tivoli, NY, 1984.

Philip, Cynthia Owen. "Fall's Fairest Apple," About Town, Tivoli, NY, Fall, 1998

Ruttenber, E.M. *Indian Tribes of Hudson's River to 1700. Saugerties,* NY, Hope Farm Press, 1992 (original, 1872).

St. John's Low Dutch Reformed Church: 200th Anniversary, 1788-1988, Upper Red Hook, NY, St. John's Reformed Church, 1988.

"Scheme for Dividing the Greater Part of the Estate of Mrs. Margaret Livingston of Claremont" Princeton, NJ, manuscript, Edward Livingston Papers, Princeton University Firestone Library.

Seventy-fifth Anniversary: St. Sylvia's Church, Tivoli, NY, St. Sylvia's Roman Catholic Church, 1978.

Sherwood, Bruce and Clouss, Richard. "Architectural History and Historic Preservation: The Commercial District of the Village of Red Hook, New York," Millbrook, NY, Cornell Cooperative Extension, 1974.

Skaaren, Lorna. "Barrytown, New York: A Brief Social and Commercial History," Annandale, NY, Vassar College, 1983.

Smith, Edward M. *Documentary History of Rhinebeck in Dutchess County,* Rhinebeck, NY, 1881.

Smith, James H. *History of Duchess County, 1683-1882,* reprint, Interlaken, NY, Heart Of The Lakes Press, 1980.

Souvenir Booklet, Ninetieth Anniversary, Free Church of St. John the Evangelist, 1874-1964, Barrytown, NY, 1964.

The Great Estates Region of the Hudson River Valley, Tarrytown, NY, Historic Hudson Valley Press, 1998.

The Livingston Legacy, Three Centuries of American History, Annandale, NY, Hudson Valley Studies, Bard College, 1986.

Thomas, Lately. *The Astor Orphans: A Pride of Lions,* Albany, NY, Washington Park Press, Ltd., 1999.

Wiles, Richard. *Tivoli Revisited: A Social History,* Rhinebeck, NY, Moran Printing, 1981.

Newspapers

The Republican Herald, Poughkeepsie, NY, various editions from 1811 to 1814
The Red Hook Weekly Journal, Red Hook, NY, various editions from 1858-1865, 1917
The Red Hook Advertiser, Red Hook, NY, 1923, 1950, 1939 etc.
The Red Hook Times, Red Hook, NY, 1919 etc.
"The Red Hook Centennial," The Register Star, August 18,1994.
"The Chanler Clambake," The New York Times, August, 1906.
The Tivoli Times, Tivoli, NY, various editions from 1917.